What people are saying about

INVENTION

"You were born to change the world. You know that, right? *Invention*, written in the heart of Silicon Valley, is a super, startling, step-by-step guide for Christian men ready to rise up and join the real change-the-world movement—the one launched 2,000 years ago. This book is a blueprint for how to discover our God-given identities and engage life with energy and courage."

Eric Metaxas
New York Times bestselling author of *Bonhoeffer*,
Nationally syndicated radio host of *The Eric Metaxas Show*

"This book is for anyone who loves God and senses there is more to life than work and busyness. *Invention* will help you find that more, even in the ordinary moments, so your life may become extraordinary."

John Ortberg
Bestselling author of *The Life You've Always Wanted*

"Discipleship of men is vital work—as men go, so go our families, our churches, and our communities. I believe that one of the enemy's greatest attacks on Christian men is to convince us to live in identities that are disconnected from who God says we are. *Invention* will inspire men and guide them on a journey to discover their true, God-given identities."

Kris Dolberry
Leader of LifeWay Men;
Editor of *Stand Firm*, a monthly
devotional magazine for men

"Justin Camp has written a wise book on one of the key issues men face—their identity as creations of God and new creations in Christ. *Invention* is a thought-provoking, practical, and creative book—and if you open your heart, it will change you."

John Sowers
Author of *The Heroic Path*

"*Invention* is creative and brave. It's for Christian men ready to escape the mundane, boring routine and start really living."

Jim Candy
Church planter at Ascent Community Church;
Author of *Can I Ask That?*

"Justin Camp gets men. He knows how to speak to us. He's an expert at peeling back our false assurances and macho mantras and addressing our true needs with life-giving truths. *Invention* is the perfect antidote to the 'quiet desperation' most modern men feel. I hope many men will read this book and discover the fuller, more meaningful life Jesus promised them."

Drew Dyck
Senior editor, CTPastors.com;
Author of *Yawning at Tigers*

Break Free
from the Culture
Hell-Bent on
Holding
You Back

INVENTiON

JUSTIN CAMP

DAVID C COOK

transforming lives together

INVENTION
Published by David C Cook
4050 Lee Vance Drive
Colorado Springs, CO 80918 U.S.A.

Integrity Music Limited, a Division of David C Cook
Brighton, East Sussex BN1 2RE, England

The graphic circle C logo is a registered trademark of David C Cook.

The website addresses recommended throughout this book are offered as a
resource to you. These websites are not intended in any way to be or imply an
endorsement on the part of David C Cook, nor do we vouch for their content.

Unless otherwise noted, all Scripture quotations are taken from ESV® Bible
(The Holy Bible, English Standard Version®), copyright © 2001 by Crossway,
a publishing ministry of Good News Publishers. Used by permission. All
rights reserved. Scripture quotations marked KJV are taken from the King
James Version of the Bible. (Public Domain.); THE MESSAGE. Copyright
© by Eugene H. Peterson 1993, 2002. Used by permission of NavPress. All
rights reserved. Represented by Tyndale House Publishers, Inc.; NIV are taken
from THE HOLY BIBLE, NEW INTERNATIONAL VERSION®, NIV®
Copyright © 1973, 1978, 1984, 2011 by Biblica, Inc.® Used by permission. All
rights reserved worldwide; NKJV are taken from the New King James Version®.
Copyright © 1982 by Thomas Nelson. Used by permission. All rights reserved.

Library of Congress Control Number 2019946238
ISBN 978-0-8307-8102-7
eISBN 978-1-4347-1265-3

The Team: Michael Covington, Rachael Stevenson,
Paul J. Pastor, Nick Lee, Susan Murdock
Cover Design: Connie Gabbert

Printed in the United States of America
First Edition 2017

1 2 3 4 5 6 7 8 9 10

081519-KEP

TO JACKSON AND OLIVER
AND THE SONS GOD LOVES

THEN THE LORD GOD FORMED THE MAN OF DUST FROM THE
GROUND AND BREATHED INTO HIS NOSTRILS THE BREATH
OF LIFE, AND THE MAN BECAME A LIVING CREATURE.

— AN ACCOUNT FROM MOSES

I DO NOT ASK THAT YOU TAKE THEM OUT OF THE WORLD,
BUT THAT YOU KEEP THEM FROM THE EVIL ONE. THEY ARE
NOT OF THE WORLD, JUST AS I AM NOT OF THE WORLD.

— A PRAYER OF JESUS

CONTENTS

BEFORE YOU START

This book is built around seven nano-histories—brief profiles of seven inventors who lived and worked during the Industrial Revolution. These sections are meant to engage your curiosity and interest but also to enrich the examination of your own God-given identity. Each one opens with a short piece of creative nonfiction. Because many details from the lives of these fascinating men have been lost, I reimagined certain scenes from their lives, reconstructing them in ways that reflect the essence of actual events or qualities of their character.

More importantly, though, the book is stocked with sections entitled "Switch On." These sections turn the focus to you. If you're serious about breaking free into your true, God-given identity, these sections are "must-do." If you engage in the exercises found there, you'll discover much about yourself, your life, and your Inventor.

I promise.

Justin Camp
San Francisco Peninsula

FLESH AND BLOOD AND BURNOUT

I CAME SO THEY CAN HAVE REAL AND ETERNAL LIFE,
MORE AND BETTER LIFE THAN THEY EVER DREAMED OF.
(JOHN 10:10 THE MESSAGE)

● ● ●

A man sits in his kitchen. Elbow on the counter, forehead resting on the thumb and fingers of his left hand. He holds a cereal spoon in his right. A phone lies next to the bowl. He uses his right pinkie to scroll through the news, trying not to drip milk on the screen.

Elections in far-off places, a war trying to wind down, wildfires—even these stories are a welcome escape.

Mornings are tough. It's inertia that keeps him moving these days. An object in motion … his internal drive is gone, his passion too. His life has turned into steady advance toward some unseen wall: head down, don't think about it.

He's gotten good at the grind. And he's getting good at acting like everything's just fine.

But he's getting weary too.

3

Pulling out of his driveway, he can barely remember any details from the walk he just took. Two blocks and back, dropping off a first grader. The board meeting is in an hour, and his mind is always turning—churning—on work.

And, in the back of it all, there are questions … and a slight, edgeless gloom.

Is this what life's supposed to be?

The board meeting goes well. Good guys; a new team. The slides projected on the screen are positive, arrows in the right directions. They've closed a few important deals. Is it going to be enough?

He stops for a *barbacoa* burrito on the way back to the office. Sits by himself at a counter near the window. Lots of hot sauce. Another few minutes of escape, distracting himself from the distraction of the food with the ever-present screen. *Come on.* He swipes through articles about college football and the opening of the NBA season.

In the car, waiting for a light to change, the questions return, softly.

Is this all my life's going to be about?

Back at a conference table, he's got meetings with new companies, one after the other—potential new investments. He keeps them to an hour each. They invigorate a bit. Optimism, passion. Not his anymore, *theirs*. But it's something.

At his desk, he works through emails in the late afternoon sun. Every time he hits "send"—every time his mind breaks focus—the questions creep back.

Is this really what I want for my life?

Coming through the front door, later than promised, he's worn. Hungry again. He needs only a few minutes to take down all the food under the foil. And then he goes to the fridge for a bit more.

The two youngest are already asleep, but he helps his wife put their oldest son to bed. "These kids are amazing," he says. Goodness and joy (and exasperation). Bedtimes never go smoothly. And his voice gets loud so easily these days. And the tension in the room gets thick.

But when the two meet on the couch, minutes later, the strain eases. She leans against him. He tells her she's amazing too.

As usual, though, they leave much unsaid, much unaddressed.

After a show, after a kiss, after too-few minutes reading, he falls into bed—and the questions come again, *full-on*. They tumble in the dark and still.

What's wrong? Nothing. I guess. But something is wrong. Isn't it?

Sometime after midnight, his mind slows enough to slip into sleep.

● ● ●

This was me. Bewildered. Burned-out. Brokenhearted. And it might be you.

Or, for you, right now, maybe there's no question ... you know *exactly* what's wrong. I've been there too.

Maybe you're facing a crushing loss—of a job or a career, of financial security, of a loved one or a marriage. Maybe you're struggling to finish school. Or land a job after graduation. Or to keep one, long after. Maybe you're struggling to get a career started. To find your place. Or maybe the place you *have* found—this career you've gotten yourself into—is never going to be the right one. Or maybe you're facing addiction. Too much work ... or escape. Flesh on a screen. Medication from a bottle or a pipe.

You know who you are. You know how you hurt. How the questions haunt you. Questions of potential and greater things.

We're in this together. Only the details are different.

● ● ●

I grew up near Silicon Valley's geographical center. For college, though, I went south. For law school, east. Then a short time on Wall Street. A young lawyer rushing through halls and conference rooms, trying his best to close mergers and acquisitions. It was a heady time, the late 1990s, at Cravath, Swaine & Moore, a big corporate law firm.

Now, Cravath is a pretty cool place. The men and women there represent the likes of DuPont, DreamWorks, IBM, Starbucks—but it's an old firm too. It has history. During the Industrial Revolution, it represented Samuel Morse (the inventor of the single-wire telegraph and Morse code); Cyrus McCormick (the mechanical reaper); Elias Howe (the sewing machine); Charles Goodyear (vulcanized rubber); and even Thomas Edison, the dean of all American inventors.

I'd chosen law because of my mother, who I love very much. She thought I'd make a good lawyer—and said so a few times while I was growing up. I had a talent for arguing, I think. Mostly with her, I guess.

I'd chosen Cravath, though, because of the competitive culture of law school. From it, I extracted this not-so-subtle advice: to go to the best firm that would take me. So, at the end of a full day of interviews at Worldwide Plaza in Manhattan, when the hiring partner gave me an offer, I took it.

I wasn't the best lawyer at Cravath, not by a long shot. But I was as good as any of them at *acting* as if everything was fine … great, in fact. It didn't always feel great. Sometimes it felt very ungreat. But our culture told me—the voices *I* was listening to, at least—that I was right where I should be. They told me I'd found what I should be doing with my life.

But if that was the truth, why did I feel so … *this*?

Something was off, I can see that now. I was anxious. I was just beginning to feel that faint, hard-to-get-a-hold-of gloom. I had plenty of confidence, but nearly all of it was an act. And when questions began to emerge, I just pushed them away. I figured that was what life was supposed to be—exciting in some ways, but confusing and unfulfilling in others. Deals I worked on showed up on the front page of the *Wall Street Journal*. That was cool—so I just ignored a nagging feeling that I might actually be in the wrong place.

Man up. Head down. The inner voice said. Every day.

My relationship with God wasn't great. My wife, Jennifer, and I went to church sometimes, but we didn't belong to one. We weren't in community. I prayed some—but my focus was on my career. I spent many Sundays in the office.

About when the millennium turned, my father asked a question. He wondered if I'd consider joining him, back in California. He's a technologist, to the core. He loves the next big thing. And he's wired, too, for investing and taking risks. So, we started kicking around the idea of starting a small venture capital firm.

It made sense. It felt like the change I needed, especially professionally. And things were booming in the Bay Area. Everyone, it seemed, was heading there—my home—to start internet companies.

On top of that, it wasn't just my father back on the West Coast; the rest of our families were there too. And if we were going to start a family ourselves, it would be good to be closer to them.

So we came home. And for the next fifteen years, I raced up and down the San Francisco Peninsula, investing in high-tech startups.

Now, working with my father was a great gift—no question. But it wasn't long before that subtle gloom returned, with those still-unanswered questions. Just like before, life was exciting in some ways, but confusing and unfulfilling in others. I got to invest in some amazing people and some exciting businesses. That was cool. So, again, I tried to ignore that by-then familiar nagging—that this might not be my place either.

We joined a great church in Menlo Park. We heard some helpful teaching. But we still weren't in community—not really. I had no idea who I was—not at all, actually. I sure knew who I *should* be. Culture told me, all the time. And I listened, all the time.

Head down. Grind.

Whenever the stress and burnout spiked, I turned to food. Watching sports. Internet pornography. Escape.

"Man up"?

Man down. This was not the life God intended.

• • •

God creates with passion and precision ... and *purpose*—just like those great inventors, those long-ago clients of Cravath.

When God set the foundations of the world, he dreamed. He made plans. He "formed" our constituent parts and "knitted" them together (Ps. 139:13). We were "fearfully and wonderfully made," just like King David—"intricately woven in the depths of the earth" (vv. 14–15). And then, with great anticipation—just as he did with the first man—God "breathed" into us life (Gen. 2:7).

We're his beloved creations, made with painstaking care and can't-miss-this intentionality—for us and for our lives. We all are— in common. And we each are—uniquely.

So, why the disconnect? Between the life we're meant for and the life we're living?

• • •

You know the life I mean.

Deeply, we long for confidence, because we're designed to *be* confident—confident in *who* we are, *where* we are, and *why* we are. Confident we have a place, a position in this world; a purpose and part to play in its story.

But mostly, we aren't. We feel unsure. Undistinguished. Sometimes it feels like God's made a mistake. Left something out. So, we cover that pain up with whatever is convenient. We resolve to work harder. We spend too much time at the office or too much on the road—to feel like we're keeping up. Or, we just numb our sense of inadequacy. We turn to alcohol, drugs, sex. We compete, or become complacent.

I know you feel you have to prove yourself, every day. *You don't.*

Deeply, we long for significance, because we're designed to do work that matters. We're designed for assignment, to be necessary parts of something larger than ourselves. We're designed for adventure, to take big risks toward worthy goals.

But we've been taught to be fearful and careful. So, we try to control everything. And we mostly just focus on minimizing risk, avoiding pain, surviving. We've forgotten what it's like to take real risks. We wonder if there are any worthy goals that need big risks anymore.

I know how you feel restless, underutilized. *You are.*

Deeply, we long for joy, because we were made for it. We're designed for wholeness and fullness. For freedom. We're designed to move through life with intention.

But mostly we're just busy and worn-out. Our lives are filled, but not *full.* Work is work. And there's so little time to rest, to restore, to do anything we love to do. So our senses have dulled. We don't smell the trees, the rain when it comes, the wood smoke. We've come to dread Monday morning and barely feel the freedom of a Saturday afternoon anymore.

I know how it feels like something's been lost. *Something has.*

Deeply, we long for good, strong relationships with God, because we're designed for them—for their intimacy and protection and strength. We're designed to laugh, to pray, and be ourselves with Him. We're meant to be known, all the way—and be loved still. We're designed to walk with him and work with him and know him, right back.

But mostly we just keep to ourselves. Reluctant to drop defenses. Fearful we'll hear something we won't like. Fearful we might not be good enough. Fearful we might be diverted from our goals. Unwilling to trust. So, we isolate further.

I know how it feels like something's got to give. *Something does.*

● ● ●

You know that sense that something's wrong? You know that feeling that you might be made for more than what you're living now?

Well … you're right. Something *is* wrong. You *are* made for more—a lot more.

And that disconnect? It's because God's purposes for us go beyond this broken, fallen world. He's made us for something bigger and better. He's made us for a world *restored*—perfect and eternal. And it's simply not yet come. This one's not yet been restored. It will be. Jesus' work has begun. And he'll finish it. But as of now, it's only partially done.

So, here we are. In a world we're not made for.

What's even more, for now, this world "lies in the power of the evil one" (1 John 5:19). Jesus rules us—you and me—his followers, and he'll rule the world to come. But, for now, right now, Satan holds sway.

And we're designed by God to join Jesus in his work of restoring things—to do our parts in pulling this world out of crisis. It's a tremendous gift and profound honor—but the evil one hates it. For the very last act of restoration will be his overthrow. And, as the ones through whom Jesus works on earth, by the power of his Holy Spirit, Satan's scared of us.

He's scared of you. And he's right to be.

But he's not standing by, either. No, he's set the culture of this world against us. He uses culture as a weapon—a weapon to defend the current order. And here's how he does it: he promulgates a set of lies, "for he is a liar and the father of lies" (John 8:44). He disseminates them into and through our culture. He shapes it—in the hope that it will shape us.

He's clever. He's motivated.

For he knows, when and if we discover *true identity*—who we're made to be and what we're made for, by God—then we also discover *true* confidence, significance, joy, relationship. We discover what Jesus promised: more and better life than we ever dreamed of.

But we also discover *impact*—we discover exactly how we're meant to do our parts to restore this world, and uniquely where. And so, Satan knows, when we discover true identity, we become dangerous.

So, he's hell-bent on thwarting us. He pummels us, again and again, with lies—telling us who to be and what to do. His false messages are everywhere. And they're insidious, because they don't sound so bad … at first, at least.

But, of course, if we believe them, if we follow them, they work to hold us back—from life, from goodness. They debilitate us—keep us unsure of ourselves, merely surviving, tired and underutilized, isolated. And, eventually, they lead us to our deaths.

So, we're here. In a world screaming for redemption, with a vicious enemy, with the odds stacked against us—against us ever living the way our God designed us to live.

Things look grim. And that's mighty good news for men like you and me—men built for opposition, men just itching for an honest challenge.

We're here. Where finding ourselves is fighting back. Where thinking differently, where *living differently*, is the best kind of rebellion—faithfulness to our true King.

● ● ●

A few years ago, I'd finally had enough. Nearly a decade after Jenn and I had come back out West, a desire grew in my heart—to stop trying to *man up*. And another one did too—the desire to turn toward God.

He placed those desires, he increased them—but, then, I finally did my part.

I surrendered. I began to let God fill in my blanks. I allowed my Inventor to begin to tell me why I was, what I was, who I was.

And it changed everything.

It can for you too.

• • •

"I came so they can have real and eternal life, more and better life than they ever dreamed of" (John 10:10 THE MESSAGE).

Jesus said that. And the "they" he's referring to is us. "They" is me. *"They" is you.*

This book is an invitation. Join me and a small band of renegades and revolutionaries, change-makers and troublemakers—men who don't accept the world as it is, because they know they're made for something better. It's an invitation, just for you. It's a guidebook to begin living. It'll help you see the lies that obscure. It'll help you reconnect with God and find the truths of your identity.

It won't be easy. It'll be so much better than that.

002

PINE AND PAINT AND FELLOWSHIP

The place has dark wood floors, plank walls, and high white ceilings. The air smells of smoke and machine oil. Fumes drift through a maze of motion and noise—a bustling office, a library, and then the machine shop. The shop is amazing—jammed with all kinds of anvils, forges, lathes, drills, and other machines, each steam-driven by an ingenious web of leather belts lacing their way through the building. Men work everywhere—shouting, laughing, and occasionally nursing cuts and bruises to fingers and hands.

Upstairs is one long room, dark wood and white paint too. It's organized around wood tables and workbenches, covered with magnifying glasses, microscopes, glass beakers, and crucibles, all kinds of gear and bits of apparatus. Wooden chairs and iron stools are pulled up or pushed away. Walls between bright sash windows are lined with shelves holding thousands of bottles, rainbows of glass and chemicals.

And through it all, a man paces. His hands are grimy and acid-stained; his hair disheveled. His face, quick and changeable, is streaked with ash and grease and dirt. His eyes sparkle and penetrate. Around him swirl machinists, mathematicians, physicists, chemists, draftsmen, and glassblowers—and he directs them all. He jokes, he corrects, he even sings.

"Once," a workman says, having to shout a bit over all the noise, "he locked the doors for two days ... until we solved this customer's problem ... until we got the purchase order filled." This is directed to some reporters in from New York, gathered and waiting for a chance to interview the man who would do such a thing.

That man stops his stride, way across the room, amid the chaos. His hand rests on a workbench for a moment. He looks lost in thought. Far away, in his mind. Preoccupied with some problem, no doubt.

But after a moment, he's back. His eyes come back into focus. He takes a long survey of the entire room, finally seeing the newspapermen for the first time. He straightens and makes his way over.

This is Menlo Park, New Jersey, and the man is Thomas Edison.

● ● ●

In the 1870s, while still in his midtwenties, Edison was living in a row house in nearby Newark. He'd been working odd jobs, including that of a telegraph operator. He'd done some inventing too—a stock ticker machine and an electric vote recorder—but only in his spare time. But he'd made a decision—he was going all in. He was going to devote everything to the work of inventing.

The world was in the midst of a great age of invention. It was the second phase of the Industrial Revolution, and Newark had established itself as a hub of industry: iron, leather, shipping. The city was also a center of innovation. A pioneering plastics factory had just opened in the city. But as its population swelled, like many large cities of the time, Newark became overcrowded and a bit hazardous. What it lacked in modern sanitation, it made up for in grime.

The age suited Edison. He was ambitious and impatient. He opened his first workshop in a rented factory building in the bustling, bursting city. In there, he and a few employees worked long hours to improve the very kind of telegraphic gear he'd used as an operator. But he soon wanted to expand his operation, and for that he would need more room—and perhaps a more peaceful location.

So in 1876 he bought thirty-four acres out in the New Jersey countryside, in a place called Menlo Park. It was quiet and unpolluted—but also an easy trip to New York City or Philadelphia. The main line of the Pennsylvania Railroad bisected the nearly nonexistent town and the "Pennsy" rumbled through on a regular basis.

In Menlo Park, Edison hit his stride. He was bold and daring. He knew what he wanted to do with his life, and he had a sense for how to do it. He built an impressive, state-of-the-art workshop atop a hill overlooking the countryside and the train station. He called it his Invention Factory.

And from that shop, he pushed the human race forward.

Over the next five years, Edison and his men did things people thought could never be done. They created wondrous things. They invented things unique and novel, and they upgraded things that others had invented, making them better and cheaper.

Edison applied for about 400 of his 1,093 patents while working out of that Menlo Park workshop, including a couple of his best: the phonograph and the first commercially viable electric light bulb.

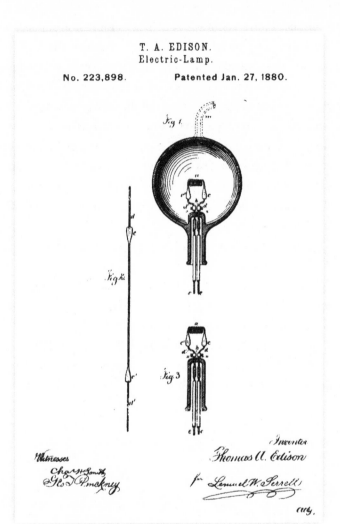

U.S. Patent N⁰ 223,898
Electric-Lamp

L i E :

"YOU'VE GOT THIS."

You've been told: *real men are self-made. They're independent. They don't need anyone. In any situation, they can handle themselves. They can handle anything. When life gets tough, they do what they need to. They work harder. Longer. They escape when they need to. Why? Because they have to—they know no help is coming, and that's just fine with them.*

You're one of these men. You're on your own—but that's okay. You've got this.

These are lies, and they're holding you back. **Think different.**

● ● ●

The mystique and mythology of the self-made man cemented into Western culture during the nineteenth century. Self-made men, people began to proclaim, shaped themselves, their lives, into whatever they wanted. With enough hard work, imagination, initiative, *anything* was possible.

"No boy, however lowly—the barefoot country boy, the humble newsboy, the child of the tenement—need despair," declared John D. Rockefeller. "I see in each of them infinite possibilities. They have but to master the knack of economy, thrift, honesty, and perseverance, and success is theirs."[1]

If a man can just find his bootstraps, all that's required for success is a lifetime of pulling himself up by them.

The self-made man became an essential American figure. Edison and Rockefeller embodied it, and they became American heroes—as did Benjamin Franklin and Abraham Lincoln before them, and Henry Ford and Walt Disney after. The figure shows up more recently in the stories of men like Ronald Reagan, Sam Walton, Steve Jobs, Bill Gates, and Barack Obama. Their stories are told and retold. Their biographies become models of self-made upward mobility. Models, we all learn, that boys and men should emulate.

So we try. (I sure did.)

If we want something, we go after it. If we want to do something, we do it. If we lack talent or skill, we figure it's just a question of effort: more is needed. We convince ourselves we can accomplish anything.

For a while, at least.

You see, the problem is when we do this, we're trying to live a myth. Because no one is self-made. No one.

We're God-made.

That's the beautiful reality. But it's a reality we miss when we examine the lives and accomplishments of men we admire but don't look for God too.

Do you want to know something? Even Edison did not make Edison.

When we look just at the man, we miss his Maker standing behind and above him. It was God, after all, who wired the curiosity, tenacity, restlessness, irreverence, and everything else that made him the inventor he was. Edison had nothing that God did not give him—and neither do you or I.

If we miss this reality, we miss everything. Because, while Edison's achievements are interesting and impressive, they all but disappear when measured against the mighty movements of God. And all of a sudden, the importance of being "self-made" shrivels in light of living according to true purpose, deepest identity.

And what we're going to learn—here, now—is how this beautiful reality is real for each of us too ... *and why we'd be absolutely crazy not to choose relationship with our Maker.*

● ● ●

Edison's passion for inventing is just a pale reflection of God's heart for creating. Edison dreamed and designed and built things, because that's what God does. God just does it on an unfathomably larger scale—the scale of worlds, of geologic ages, of human lives.

Once, while searching for a filament for his light bulb, Edison made a surprising discovery. "Sitting one night in his laboratory reflecting on some of the unfinished details, Edison began abstractedly rolling between his fingers a piece of compressed lampblack until it had become a slender thread."[2] Lampblack is the fine black powder from kerosene smoke that collects on the glass chimneys of oil lamps.

Looking down at the thread, it struck the inventor that it might be exactly what he'd been looking for. So, he tried it.

And the entire world changed.

Within a few months, Menlo Park was lit by twenty-five electric lamps. Edison had taken something dark—to all appearances useless—and turned it into something *beautiful*. He brought light out of darkness. And multitudes came to see.

Long before that night, God too took something dark and seemingly useless and created something beautiful, something also meant to radiate light. When God created Adam he "formed the man of dust from the ground and breathed into his nostrils the breath of life, and the man became a living creature" (Gen. 2:7).

● ● ●

We don't make ourselves. No one does. It's not a matter of trying to be smarter or working harder or more efficiently. It's simply this: God is the one who dreamed us up, who made plans for us before we were even born.

While our choices matter—and we can take some credit for hard work and grit—we have nothing without God. We're *his* workmanship. It's his hand that wrought us—not our own.

So the figure of the self-made man is a myth—but it's worse. It's a counterfeit too. It looks right, sounds good, but it deceives. It lies to us. It convinces us to become men who go it alone, men who don't know our Maker. Men whose only option when things get tough is to *man up*.

But that's just not how God designed us. He designed us not for isolation and self-reliance—but for God-relationship and God-reliance.

Of all that God's made, only we humans have the capacity for relationship with him. Only we are able to know him—to know the One "who made heaven and earth, the sea, and all that is in them" (Ps. 146:6). And too often we take that astonishing fact way too lightly. It should be the thing in our lives we hold most dear—not our smarts or success or anyone else's.

> Thus says the LORD: "Let not the wise man boast in his wisdom, let not the mighty man boast in his might, let not the rich man boast in his riches, but let him who boasts boast in this, that he understands and knows me, that I am the LORD who practices steadfast love, justice, and righteousness in the earth." (Jer. 9:23–24)

We must avail ourselves of this unique and awesome functionality of ours, this ability to know him. We all have it—but what matters is that we actually *use* it.

In this chapter, we'll learn *why*. In this book, we'll learn *how*.

● ● ●

In 1884 a twenty-seven-year-old Serbian stepped off a steamship and into the jam-packed streets of New York City. The man had skills—both mechanical and electrical. He had a sharp mind, a splendid imagination, and a photographic memory. And he'd come to meet Thomas Edison.

This man was Nikola Tesla. In Paris, he had been working for the Continental Edison Company, where he had impressed one of Edison's close personal friends. That man offered an introduction. Meeting Edison, Tesla knew, was an opportunity he couldn't pass up. So he sold his possessions and set off across the Atlantic.

The two men met. Edison hired Tesla to work in the Edison Machine Works—a new factory constructed on a rough street, amongst the teeming tenements of Manhattan's Lower East Side. Edison needed a factory that could keep up with the raw demand for electrical illumination. Now everyone wanted electric lights. So the world now needed massive machines, things like jumbo dynamos, which could supply electricity on a wide scale.

Why did Tesla sell everything and sail to America? Because he wanted to know Edison—to work for him and beside him. He wanted to be where the action was. He wanted to work on things that were exciting, things that mattered. He wanted to tackle tough problems and learn. He sought truth and wanted to make an impact on the world—and he didn't want to do it alone.

Tesla would go on to become a celebrated inventor in his own right. But it must have been an amazing thing for the young Tesla to get personal access to the world-famous Edison, to be given the opportunity for a relationship—even if it was short-lived.

But the thing is, what Edison offered Tesla comes nowhere close—nowhere even remotely close—to what God offers us. In him, we have the colossal and incomprehensible honor of a relationship with our Inventor, the Most High God.

We're invited to get to know, to work for and beside someone who, in every way imaginable, dwarfs Thomas Edison and every other human. Even the richest, the most successful, the most accomplished. He dwarfs them all—and even that's a monstrous understatement.

When we get to know him, we're invited out of the lie that we have to or should or even can figure out life on our own. We move from self-reliance (which, in all honesty, is not very much of anything) into God-relationship and God-reliance (which is very much of everything).

We're invited into where the *real* action is. We get to be part of the most exciting and significant work in the entire world—*in the history of the entire world.* We get to tackle tough problems—ours and other people's—and we get to do it standing right at God's side, God Almighty. We get access to his truth, his infinite wisdom. And we get to make our impact on the world—an impact magnified, multiplied by the most powerful force in the universe.

We *cannot* miss this chance.

● ● ●

For all the glory and wonder, though, there's nothing easy about making this choice, this shift—and it's even harder to do it consistently. Our culture has programed our beliefs and our habits—and our old ways die hard.

Think for a moment, where does your mind go first when the shock of something awful hits—like when you get scary financial news or an unwelcome diagnosis, when you lose a job or tear a relationship? To God? For help? Where does it go when something awesome happens—a major success at work or an unexpected blessing? To God? To express gratitude?

Or does it go somewhere else?

I don't know how many times I've done this, but it's a lot. I'm anxious; I'm working through a problem by talking with Jenn; at some point she suggests we pray, suggests we ask for God's help—and I push back. Usually, ultimately, either we don't pray or I pray through gritted teeth. Whatever the words are, the heart's always the same: *I've got this.* I want control. I want to say who I am, what I'm supposed to do, how I work best. *I don't need help.*

I don't *want* to need help. But I do.

I've only recently been able to accept that. I've only recently been able to loosen my grip on my fantasy of control. I guess enough has happened. I've made enough mistakes, damaged enough relationships. I've spent enough of my life devoting myself to a life and work that, according to our culture, should have given me everything I long for—life to the full. They didn't. They don't. And only when it felt like I was drowning in discontent, only when I had to use sheer will to wrench myself out of bed on weekday mornings, did the idea finally occur to me.

Maybe I haven't got this.

And *that's* when I was finally able to surrender. And *that's* when I turned to God.

● ● ●

When we live as if we make ourselves, we compartmentalize. We attempt to live different realities at different times. We accept God's position and presence and power on Sunday mornings at church. But the rest of the week, at home and at work, we try to live self-made, as if the God of the universe isn't really right there with us, standing behind us and above us, beside us and inside us. We try to live as if God just isn't all that relevant to our goals and all the things we need to get done. (I tried to live that way.)

And do you know why that doesn't work?

Because none of us is man enough to handle life on our own—even portions of it.

We're in over our heads. All of us.

And that's perfectly okay. It's right.

None of us is man enough because we aren't designed to be. We aren't designed to *go it alone*—because we never have been alone, we never are alone, and we'll never be alone, ever. Jesus told his disciples, he tells us, "Behold, I am with you always, to the end of the age" (Matt. 28:16–20). He promised his Spirit will dwell with us and be in us "forever" (John 14:16–17). And that's why the self-made figure, this counterfeit, takes us so far off track.

It convinces us to violate our God-designed, God-given, *with-God* nature.

We think we know what we're made for. We don't. Our Maker does. No one understands us like the One who designed us, made us—not by stamping us out on some heavenly production line, but as handcrafted, irreplaceable masterworks.

Because God is Inventor, and we are his inventions, there's a gulf between what he knows and what we do—and it's vast. It's so big, in fact, we can't comprehend it—"his understanding is beyond measure" (Ps. 147:4–5). "His understanding is unsearchable" (Isa. 40:28). He sees everything, knows everything, and can do anything. "'I am the Alpha and the Omega,' says the Lord God, 'who is and who was and who is to come, the Almighty'" (Rev. 1:8).

Dallas Willard, the great philosopher and provocateur, wrote this: "Today we think people are smart who make light bulbs and computer chips and rockets out of 'stuff' already provided! He made 'the stuff!'"[3]

All things that God is, he is infinitely. His love, his power, *his knowledge*—they're without end. We'll never approach his level of understanding, even when what we're talking about is understanding *ourselves*. Trying to live self-made, self-reliant lives is doomed from the start, therefore, because it's trying to live an impossibility. It's denying the source of all things that make not only our lives, but *existence itself*, possible.

No wonder our lives are fraught with sadness and suffering—wrong fits, false starts, and broken parts. No wonder we're unsure of ourselves, merely surviving, tired, underutilized, isolated. No wonder we're sad, lonely, addicted, divorced, thinking late at night, *Is this it? Is this all there is?*

No. Of course it's not all there is. What we're feeling is simply the friction of God's reality against our paltry attempts at finding meaning apart from our Maker. Living into a lie has simply begun to unmake our lives.

But living into the truth will remake them.

With God, we have everything we need. We're qualified. Ready to go. With him, we can find what we're made for: confidence, significance, joy, relationship, excitement, adventure, peace, rest, and restoration.

We're going to learn how ... *all of it.*

● ● ●

It was not *all inventing all the time* with Edison. He apprenticed men too. They came from all over the world to work for him in his workshop. Edison called these men his "muckers." He chose them. He taught them. He pushed them. He laughed and ate with them. He liked being with them, and they with him—most of the time, at least. He cultivated an environment of rough-and-tumble camaraderie—to bring his employees together, but also to provide relief and release from the long hours and hard work.

Charles Clarke, assistant to Edison, described things this way:

> Laboratory life with Edison was a strenuous but joyous life for all, physically, mentally, and emo-tionally. We worked long night hours during the week, frequently to the limit of human endur-ance ... he breathed a little community of kindred spirits ... enthusiastic about their work, expectant of great results; moreover often loudly emphatic in joke and vigorous in action.[4]

The men pulled pranks and competed in games and tests of strength. They drank beer, chewed tobacco, ate midnight meals together, and held roisterous sing-alongs. Edison even had a pipe organ installed on the second floor of the Invention Factory.

THE INVENTION FACTORY
MENLO PARK, NEW JERSEY, 1880

Edison and his muckers did historic work, created important things. Perhaps the single most astonishing thing created in the Invention Factory, though, was the place itself—the environment, the relationships, the apprenticeships, the men. The workshop, nearly a living organism. Many muckers went on to make significant contributions of their own—to science, research, and engineering. It was a place where many men were formed and some transformed.

• • •

Not only are we God's inventions, we're his apprentices too. For just as Edison chose his muckers, God chooses us—to join him, to grow and deepen our relationships, to help him as he remakes the world through the work of Jesus. "You did not choose me, but I chose you" (John 15:16). And his work of forming our physical bodies is not the end of his creation work. Later on, when we begin to follow his perfect invention, Jesus Christ, God picks up his tools and creates again—new men and new lives.

When we make the decision to follow Jesus, he reinvents us by the power of the Holy Spirit. He re-forms us—"If anyone is in Christ, he is a new creation" (2 Cor. 5:17). When the apostle Paul wrote, "We are his workmanship," he was referring to this *re*-invention—"in Christ Jesus" (Eph. 2:10).

This reinvention isn't figurative. It's real and complete. We're completely overhauled, made new.

In an instant, we become new men—men who *can* become the men God designed us to be. We become men who *can* be taught, *can* be guided, *can* be challenged and pushed, *can* be encouraged and befriended and fathered by God—we become men who *can* be apprenticed. We will spend the rest of our lives living into that reality, but our redesign is complete.

In an instant, we become God's muckers, able to learn how to be like Jesus. Able to learn how to love and serve God, our neighbors, our enemies, the entire world. The world, his workshop, becomes a place of labor, creativity, risk-taking, problem-solving.

But laughing and joking and singing too.

Work. And joy. The deepest longings of a good man's heart.

What we were made for.

● ● ●

Do you want to discover *your* true identity? Do you want to discover the plans God has for you?

Then stop trying to live a myth. Give it up. Self-made? Not even close. Made. Then, in Jesus, *remade.* Better than the very best work we could ever do on our own.

And simply keep reading. Coming chapters will guide you in how to bring God your deepest questions of identity. The right ones. In the right way.

But first, in the very next chapter, we're going to learn how to *listen.* Listen for the Inventor's voice.

SWITCH ON
"GOD MADE"
002

You're an invention of God, made in his image. You're a mucker, an apprentice to the loving God of all goodness and might. He's chosen you. He knows you, and he wants you to know him.

He wants you to know what he made you for. He's desperate for you to find purpose and significance and excitement—joy and peace and rest and restoration. And he's eager for you to make your unique impact on the world.

He wants you to join him where the action is. He wants to pull you into what he's doing in the world. His work. He has assignments for you. Waiting.

If you want all of this—or even any part—tackle the questions below. They're a first step in this crazy, wonderful process of discovery and recovery.

Consider these questions and jot down your responses.

002.1   Describe yourself. Can you do it in just a few sentences—your personality and talents, your hopes and dreams? It's hard. Try.

002.2   How would friends, acquaintances, coworkers describe you?

002.3   Have you ever taken the self-made, go-it-alone approach to life? Have you ever said to God, "I've got this"? Why?

002.4　Where would you put yourself on this spectrum, right now?

<<Self-reliant - - - - - - - - - - - - - - - - - - God-reliant>>
1　2　3　4　5　6　7　8　9　10

002.5　God wants a relationship with you—close and dynamic. He wants you to become his mucker. You are chosen. You are able. But that apprentice-ship will cost you—it might cost you everything you now hold dear. How does that make you feel?

Pray right now.

> *Jesus my King, not once did you try to go it alone. Not once did you say to your Father, "I've got this." Rather, you said, "I can do nothing on my own" (John 5:30). And so, you and your Father and the Holy Spirit changed the world—in ways infinitely bigger and better than any self-made man ever has, even the most celebrated.*
>
> *I confess I've wanted to be self-made. Independent. I've wanted to not need anyone. I've wanted to not need you. But I choose now to think differently. I choose to live like you did—knowing my Father God, depen-dent upon the Holy Spirit. I choose to live as you made me. I want to do the things you made me to do.*
>
> *Teach me. Guide me. Apprentice me into my true identity. I'm ready. Amen.*

003

NICKEL AND GLASS AND FAITH

I t's stifling. Windows of the attic workshop are thrown open, but it barely helps. The tops of the trees outside are perfectly still.

Two men are in there. One is young, barely past twenty. His sharp features fit his close-cropped hair, which is combed and slicked back. He's thin; his complexion pale—but he's focused. Intense. He's getting things set up. Fiddling with a contraption on one side of the room one moment, darting over to connect wires on the other side of the room the next.

The other man is older—patient, kind. Standing with an air of formality, ready to assist however he can.

The room has plaster walls, a floor of red tile, a ceiling with heavy beams. It used to be used for raising silkworms. Silkworms now gone, there are tables that look like they were pilfered from elsewhere in the villa. There are chairs, wooden with rush seats, and a low stool. There are tools, equipment, chemistry apparatus scattered about. Most of it secondhand and jury-rigged.

The contraption the young man is fiddling with is a jar of sorts. It sits on a table. It's coated with metal, but only halfway up. It has a large cork stuffed in its neck, and a brass rod runs from inside the jar, through the cork, and into the air a few inches above.

31

On another table, this one on the far side of the room, there's an odd-shaped glass capsule. The capsule is connected by wires to a battery and a small bell—but no wires stretch across the room. No wires connect to the jar.

Hands sweaty, the young man picks up a brass wand. On one end is a two-pronged fork. He steps to the jar, but glances back at the capsule, then to the older man.

"Okay, Mignani, ci siamo." ("Okay, Mignani, here we go.")

"Sì, ci siamo." ("Yes, here we go.")

The young man is Guglielmo Marconi. And with the aid of his family's butler, he's about to start a wireless revolution.

● ● ●

It was the 1890s. Marconi was living at Villa Griffone, his parents' estate in Pontecchio, Italy—in the country, between Venice and Bologna. His father, Giuseppe Marconi, was a businessman and an aristocrat. His mother, Annie Jameson, was the granddaughter of John Jameson, the Irish whiskey-maker.

The young Marconi had little in the way of formal education but had nonetheless gotten interested in experimenting with electromagnetism—a subject that had become the talk of scientific circles at the time. It captured him. A few years earlier, others had discovered that electrical sparks had an odd effect on metal filings. They would cling to one another but only in the presence of a spark. They'd do this even when a spark was produced some distance away. The effect is caused by electromagnetic radiation, which sparks emit—along with light (flash) and sound (pop).

Marconi was among the first, though, to dream of the possibilities that electromagnetism held for communication—which was being revolutionized by the telegraph but was limited, always limited, by *wires*.

The jar in the attic workshop was what's known as a Leyden jar. It can store static electricity and create a spark on demand—with the help of the brass wand. The capsule was a coherer—a long, narrow glass device with electrodes on either end. The electrodes penetrate the glass and nearly meet in the middle of the capsule, but not quite. In the gap, inside the capsule, there are metal filings. Marconi had settled on a mixture of metals: 95 percent nickel; 5 percent silver.

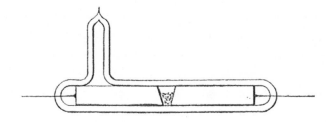

CROSS SECTION OF A COHERER

A coherer allows electrical current to flow through it, but only when electromagnetic radiation is present. When it is, the filings stick to one another and to the electrodes, completing a circuit and allowing electricity to flow—if it's also connected to a battery, of course.

In Marconi's rudimentary system, when he created a spark with his Leyden jar, the circuit rang a bell on the other side of the room … no wires.

Communication, of sorts. And at the time, a bit of a miracle.

Wireless communication became the singular goal of Marconi's life. By the summer of 1895, he'd created a system he could take outdoors. For he knew, if he could establish that his invention didn't need line-of-sight, it would be much more impactful—and much more valuable. A system needing line-of-sight requires an unobstructed straight-line path between transmitter and receiver—that is, the receiver must actually be able to see the transmitter. A system that can operate without line-of-sight can, by contrast, navigate obstacles—such as hills, mountains, and horizons.

Marconi selected a hill on the grounds of the family estate as an obstruction over which to run a test. And so, Alphonso, his brother, Mignani, their butler, and a donkey strapped with gear tramped off—across a field and over the hill. Marconi spent the next few moments … waiting. Adding to the tension, both his mother (supportive) and his father (skeptical) stood with him.

Built into his new system was a telegraph key—to generate the dots and dashes of Morse code. After Marconi had waited the agreed upon interval, he began tapping. Silence. More taps. Silence. Then … *crack*. The men on the other side of the hill fired a hunting rifle to indicate they'd heard the transmission—a mile and a half away.

Without wires, beyond sight.

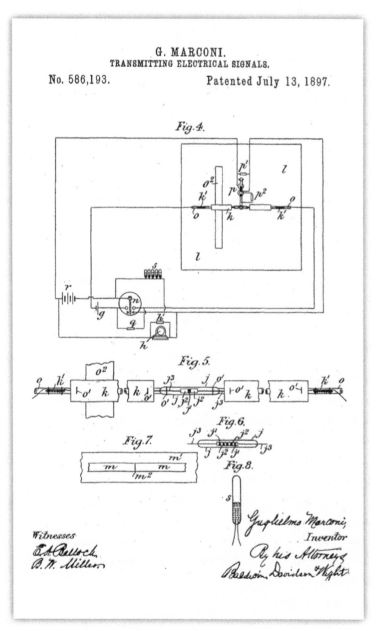

G. MARCONI.
TRANSMITTING ELECTRICAL SIGNALS.

No. 586,193.   Patented July 13, 1897.

Fig. 4.

Fig. 5.

Fig. 6.

Fig. 7.

Fig. 8.

Witnesses:

Guglielmo Marconi,
Inventor

By his Attorneys

U.S. PATENT N° 586,193
TRANSMITTING ELECTRICAL SIGNALS

LiE:

"TRUST WHAT YOU CAN SEE AND TOUCH."

You've been told: *the Bible is great. Jesus had some amazing things to say. No doubt. And it's awesome to go to church on Sundays and hear some first-class sermons. But the thing is, you have to be a bit disconnected from reality to believe that God wants to speak to you … right now. Back when the Bible was written? To those men and women? Sure. But it's a very different world today.*

Stick to what's solid and sure. Trust what you can see and touch.

These are lies, and they're holding you back. **Think different.**

• • •

Most of us live in *what's-right-in-front-of-us* mode—a presentation at work, a spreadsheet, an email, a child's sporting event, a meal out, a news report on a mobile device, a tweet, a status update, a shared photo. These things fill our minds and fill our days. We trust them. They're real. Observable.

But just because we can't see something or touch it doesn't mean it's not there—and not important.

Consider gravity, electromagnetism, the strong nuclear force, and the weak nuclear force. We can't see or touch them. But we experience their reality every day. We know they're here, doing their work, holding the cosmos together, binding together atoms … and galaxies.

Now consider God and his invisible works. We can't see or touch him either. But he's here too. And more deeply real than anything we can perceive with our everyday senses.

Marconi found him in his work with the electromagnetic force. "The more I work with the forces of Nature and sense the Divine good-will towards mankind," he said, "the more I am brought into contact with the great truth: that everything is ordered by the Lord and Giver of Life."[1]

God spoke to Marconi—not audibly, not to his physical ears, but he spoke to him. He apprenticed him. He taught him about the world, about truth, about himself.

The danger of spending too much time in what's-right-in-front-of-us mode is that it gets in the way of this. It gets in the way of everything we're trying to do here. It prevents relationship. It prevents apprenticeship. It prevents us from hearing God's voice and causes us to miss the deepest realities about our lives.

For we'll never discover true identity, we'll never discover the plans God has for us, if we get so distracted by the things of the world that we never stop to listen. He can't apprentice us into significance, joy, or anything else if we never learn to hear him.

So, everything hinges on this. Everything depends on our being able to hear the voice of our Maker. And in this chapter, we'll learn how.

● ● ●

God speaks. He wants to speak to you.

He speaks in many ways and always has. The Bible tells of him speaking sometimes in ways that actually *are* detectable by our physical senses—with an audible voice; through physical phenomena and signs; through messengers, such as angels, prophets, everyday people, even a donkey. It also shows him, though, speaking beyond our physical senses: through dreams and visions; and directly to our minds, through his Holy Spirit.

This last one has come to be called the "still small voice," and it's a seemingly preferred method of communicating. It's a primary method of *apprenticing*—so it's critical that we become adept at hearing him in this manner.

● ● ●

"Still small voice"—the words come from the story of Elijah, when the prophet was told to go out from the cave where he was hiding, because God was about to pass by:

> A great and strong wind tore the mountains and broke in pieces the rocks before the LORD, but the LORD was not in the wind. And after the wind an earthquake, but the LORD was not in the earthquake. And after the earthquake a fire, but the LORD was not in the fire. (1 Kings 19:11–13)

And after the fire, a "still small voice" came to Elijah (v. 12 KJV). God's voice. God was teaching Elijah (and us) that his voice doesn't often come as a blast or boom or blaze, but as what we might call an *inner voice*. He's teaching that when he speaks, he speaks more to our thoughts than to anything else.

Think of that—the voice of our mighty Maker, coming as a whisper. Forcing us to bend our minds, to humble ourselves to the seeming foolishness of listening *inside* for a God of impossibly great power.

When God speaks with his still small voice, he originates thoughts in our minds. But that's not hard. We can all do that. I can originate one in your mind right now by putting words on this page: *steaming cup of coffee*. With them, I've originated a thought, crystallized as a set of words, or a picture perhaps. I've directed your thinking. I've redirected the stream of thoughts flowing through your mind.

But I face limits.

To originate a thought in the mind of another, we humans need media—vibrations of vocal cords; ink on paper; pixels on screens; ones and zeros flowing through cables; waves of electromagnetic radiation. But God does not. He's already there—in our minds. If we're followers of Jesus, the Holy Spirit occupies our very beings.

And he apprentices us, leading us into an understanding of ourselves and him and his work and this world, right from that very place.

• • •

Another seemingly preferred method of communicating to us is through other people. God often uses someone willing to listen—a friend, a family member, an acquaintance—as his "agent." He directs *their* thoughts and allows them to deliver his message the rest of the way, to us.

Much of the apprenticing we'll receive during our lives will come by this second primary method—by the simple words of faithful people.

That's why being in community with other followers of Jesus is so important. And it's why reading the Bible is so important too. We can hear God's voice in Christian community, through the inspired words of friends. And we can hear his voice through Scripture. The Bible is itself, in fact, the best example we have of God's voice reaching us through intermediaries—apprenticing us, through the biblical authors, across the ages.

• • •

This is very good news. God hasn't cut us off—put us out of range—with no method of contact. But he *does* give us a choice, as he always does. He allows us to choose whether we want to learn *how* to hear him. Whether we want to be the kind of men who *want* to hear him. Whether we will enter the unseen and bring its effects back into the seen, into our everyday lives.

Do you want to do that? Do you want that kind of insight in your life?

Of course. But God's voice isn't the only unseen transmission competing for your attention, is it?

• • •

Within a decade of his breakthrough at Villa Griffone, Marconi had successfully set up a number of transmitting stations. Within a decade and a half, he was providing consistent wireless telegraph service, especially to ships in the Atlantic. But these stations were not like radio stations of today. They were more like telegraph offices, minus telegraph wires. In them, operators sent, received, and relayed telegraph traffic, wirelessly.

Imagine a Marconi operator in the early part of the twentieth century sitting in a station somewhere—maybe in the station on Cape Cod, in South Wellfleet, Massachusetts. He would have dealt with what scientists and communications engineers call *signal-to-noise ratio*. It's a measure that compares the strength of a desired signal to the level of background noise.

For our imagined operator, a desired signal would have been a message meant for his office, radio waves speeding through the sky, across land or across the seas, at nearly the speed of light. And background noise would have been all the other stuff out there in the ether, stuff he didn't care to receive. In the early days of wireless telegraphy, background noise was mostly atmospheric in nature—electromagnetic radiation naturally present in the atmosphere, primarily from lightning strikes.

Before long, however, the level of background noise giving our Marconi operator trouble would have increased dramatically—as the number of stations on land and the number of Marconi offices aboard ships proliferated.

Soon, the air was filled. Dots and dashes began to jam limited radio frequencies. And things got complicated. Transmissions began to interfere with one another.

●　●　●

We face noise too. It's been there our entire lives, a cascade of truths and lies and half-truths. Messages hit us every day—from friends, family, colleagues, the internet, television. All of which wouldn't be much of a problem if God spoke more often by unmistakable methods—a thunderous voice from the heavens perhaps. The "signal

7955. MARCONI WIRELESS STATION, SOUTH WELLFLEET, MASS.

MARCONI WIRELESS STATION
SOUTH WELLFLEET, MASSACHUSETTS, 1898

strength" of his voice would prevent it from being drowned out by the noise of the world.

But the signal strength of the methods God *does* usually use is low. Consider the still small voice. Its tone isn't dramatic; its volume isn't loud. It's never so obvious that we can't miss or mistake it. We can. We do. (I sure have.)

Or, consider the voices of faithful friends, acting as intermediaries, trying to speak God's truth into our lives. If we're not careful, we can very easily miss their encouragements or warnings, failing to distinguish them from all the other words, the everyday conversations.

So just as noise was a problem for our imagined Marconi operator, it's a problem for us too. It can stop this discovery and recovery process cold. It can prevent us from being apprenticed into true identity—into confidence, significance, joy, and relationship.

But it can be done, of course, this hearing—despite noise. Again, we just have to *choose*. Basil Pennington, a big-hearted (and big-bearded) Trappist monk, wrote this:

> God is infinitely patient. He will not push himself into our lives. He knows the greatest thing he has given us is our freedom. If we want habitually, even exclusively, to operate from the level of our own reason, He will respectfully keep silent. We can fill ourselves with our own thoughts, ideas, images, and feelings. He will not interfere.[2]

It's his nature. He takes his time. He allows us to ignore him.

But if we *choose* to listen—if we learn to listen above the noise— we will hear him, and our lives will transform.

● ● ●

There's a workshop in my father's garage. He's an electrical engineer, and his workshop is an engineer's workshop. It has two wooden workbenches. Hanging overhead is an industrial fluorescent light. On top of the larger workbench sits an oscilloscope, a variable power supply, a signal generator, a soldering iron, and a large toolbox. On the smaller workbench sits a chest—its drawers full of alligator clips, spools of wire, connectors, transistors, capacitors, resistors, LEDs, batteries, bolts, and nuts. Growing up, it was a magical place, where I could tinker and build.

Once, my dad and I built a radio. Rather than metal filings, though, we used a crystal. For a little more than a century ago, back when Marconi was still running around the world setting up his stations, other scientists discovered that crystals of certain minerals, such as galena, could detect radio waves too—and with greater sensitivity than nickel and silver.

A crystal radio is a simple device. Ours had a thick cardboard tube wrapped tight in copper wire; a thick, stiff tuner wire; a crystal detector; and an earphone. The copper-wrapped tube, along with the thick wire, allowed us to tune the radio—something users of Marconi's early systems couldn't do.

A tuner is crucial because, today, there are lots of transmitters. There are many radio stations, and my dad and I didn't want to receive all of them—especially not all at once. But we did want to receive some.

Fortunately, stations broadcast radio waves with unique characteristics, so we can tell them each apart. The tuner we built—like all tuners—allowed us to make our radio temporarily sensitive to radio waves with certain characteristics only. And, therefore, it was able to receive broadcasts from one radio station at a time.

Our tuner allowed us to pick up and pick out our desired signal from all the noise. To hear a single voice, or a single song, from the electromagnetic radiation that filled our California garage.

● ● ●

Marconi stations dealt with noise in a different way. As stations prolif-erated, they began to use "call signs." These allowed stations to iden-tify themselves to one another. Call signs were unique characteristics embedded right into every message. Operators would just listen for cer-tain ones, indicating messages meant for them. When they heard the right call sign, they would *tune in*. Everything else, they would ignore.

The use of call signs—unique identifiers—is fundamental to communication. Public telephone systems use telephone numbers; email networks use email addresses; the internet uses IP addresses. For communication to work, we must be able to identify who's speak-ing. If we cannot, things break down. Everything becomes noise.

Marconi's call signs started as two-letter identifiers, but expanded to three as more stations came online. The station from which Marconi sent the world's first transatlantic wireless message was on Table Head, a headland in Glace Bay in Nova Scotia, on the eastern coast of Canada. The call sign for that station was VAS. The station that received that message was in Poldhu, in Cornwall, on the south-west coast of England. Its call sign was 2YT.

So, if our imagined Marconi operator heard MCC, he'd know the message coming through was meant for his office, on Cape Cod. Then, if he heard VAS, he'd know Glace Bay was the station *sending* the message. Or if he heard 2YT, he'd know it was coming instead from Poldhu.

But noise wouldn't have been the only thing giving our imagined Marconi operator trouble. He might also have had to deal with mes-sages that bore false information. Consider the message that caused *The Baltimore Evening Sun* to publish the following headline on the evening of April 15, 1912: "All Titanic Passengers Are Safe."

The Titanic hit an iceberg at 11:40 p.m. on April 14. The ship slid beneath the still surface of the Atlantic at 2:20 a.m. on the morn-ing of April 15. But when the *Evening Sun*'s article ran, more than twelve hours later, it proclaimed that the "latest word received by wireless was that there was no doubt that the new White Star liner would reach port."

Messages like this, those containing false information, looked and sounded just like the ones containing truth. They were carried by the same dots and dashes; they were sent and received accurately. They were simply false.

●　　●　　●

Don't believe everything you hear.

Some voices interfere with our ability to hear God's simply by crowding it, by introducing noise—but others bear messages that are intentionally false. Dallas Willard wrote:

> Satan will not come to us in the form of an over-
> sized bat with bony wings, hissing like a snake. Very
> seldom will he assume any external manifestation
> at all. Instead he will usually, like God, come to
> us through our thoughts and our perceptions. We
> must be alert to any voice that is in contrast with
> the weight, spirit, and content of God's voice.[3]

We must be alert. It's easy to assume these thoughts are just our own—originated by us, and not by someone who wants to destroy us. Someone who's afraid of our true identities, and who wants to foist upon us as much misinformation as he can.

The story in the Bible of the husband and wife, Ananias and Sapphira, is a cautionary tale of two people who were not alert. At the time of the story, followers of Jesus were selling property and possessions and donating the proceeds to the apostles, for distribution according to need and for the good of the early Church. Ananias and Sapphira sold property too, and donated proceeds. The thing was, they lied about the sale price. They claimed to be donating *all* the proceeds from the sale. But they'd sold the property for more than they claimed, and secretly kept the difference for themselves.

The apostle Peter confronted Ananias:

"Ananias, how did Satan get you to lie to the Holy
Spirit and secretly keep back part of the price of the
field? Before you sold it, it was all yours, and after
you sold it, the money was yours to do with as you
wished. So what got into you to pull a trick like
this?" (Acts 5:3–4 THE MESSAGE)

The idea to lie—the message encouraging them to compromise
their true identities, their integrity, their character, all for a bit of
money—stood in contrast to the weight, spirit, and content of God's
voice in Scripture. It was a thought, as Peter said, originated by Satan.

Does that same enemy originate those kinds of thoughts today?
Absolutely. News stories are filled with people who've acted on them.

But really, we all do. We say stupid things—we hurt people
when we should help them heal. We spend money on stupid stuff—
on ourselves, when people need our help, desperately. We run when
we should stay. We stay when we should run. We do nothing—we lie
down when we should stand up. And we hide—we stay in the dark
when we should be the light.

The evil one sought to apprentice Ananias and Sapphira. And
they allowed him to.

Too often, so do we.

● ● ●

Jesus promises that he'll speak, that we'll hear him, and that we'll
know it's him. We'll be able to identify his voice. We'll be able to tell
it from all counterfeits:

"Truly, truly, I say to you, he who does not enter
the sheepfold by the door but climbs in by another
way, that man is a thief and a robber. But he who
enters by the door is the shepherd of the sheep. To
him the gatekeeper opens. The sheep hear his voice,

and he calls his own sheep by name and leads them out. When he has brought out all his own, he goes before them, and the sheep follow him, for they know his voice. A stranger they will not follow, but they will flee from him, for they do not know the voice of strangers." (John 10:1–5)

The sheep know the Shepherd's voice, and they flee from those that are false. The sheep are us—you and me—and Jesus is "the good shepherd" (v. 11).

Okay, so how do we know it? How do we pick out God's voice from amongst the noise and the false voices in our world? How do we *tune in*—so he can apprentice us into truth, into true character, into true identity?

Well, just as radio waves broadcast by radio stations have unique characteristics, so too does God's voice. And just as Marconi's messages bore call signs, so too do God's messages. We tune in, therefore, by learning to identify those characteristics—by learning God's call sign. And we do that by using his written word: Scripture.

You see, not all methods of hearing God are equal. Reading Scripture—the method by which we hear his voice through the biblical authors, his faithful intermediaries of old—sits above all others in terms of authority. It sits above "because Christ has endorsed its authority," explained John Stott, upper-crust Brit-cum-evangelical big shot:

> As we look back to the Old Testament, he has endorsed it. As we look forward to the New Testament, we accept it because of the apostolic witness to Christ. He deliberately chose and appointed and prepared the apostles, in order that they might have their unique apostolic witness to him.[4]

It sits above all others, said Stott, because our King said so.

Now, this method of hearing God through Scripture requires good interpretation and the work of the Spirit, of course. But with those, we have a trustworthy touchstone by which to evaluate anything and everything—including the many thoughts and messages that inundate our minds every day of our lives.

With Scripture, we can learn the unique timbre of the Shepherd's voice.

●　●　●

Remember the four basic forces of nature: gravity, electromagnetism, the strong nuclear force, and the weak nuclear force? If we can't see them, how do we know they're there? How can we be sure they're real?

Because we can see their effects. Marconi knew electromagnetic radiation was present when he created a spark, because he saw its effect on metal filings.

God's voice affects the seen world from the unseen. So, when we think we may have heard it, or when someone else thinks they have, we can simply examine the nature and the *effect* of the words that were heard. We can ask, do they fit within everything we know about God from Scripture—his nature, his love, his goodness?

Here's an example. James, the brother of Jesus, wrote, "The wisdom from above is first pure, then peaceable, gentle, open to reason, full of mercy and good fruits, impartial and sincere" (James 3:17).

When we think we've heard something, therefore, when we sense that God wants to guide or teach or shape us, we can ask ourselves, do the words we've heard fit with these things? Will the effect of the words in the world *be* those things? If they do, if they will, we can trust them. If not, we can reject them.

●　●　●

We'll get to specific questions of identity in coming chapters, but here's a practical example. This is a stream of thoughts that could have run through my mind during a time of prayer, back when I was facing massive amounts of discontent:

> God, I know you have good plans for me. But this life I'm leading, it doesn't feel right. I'm anxious much of the time. I'm working so hard, but I can never seem to break through to peace and joy. And everyone else seems to have it all together. No one else has any problems. There must be something wrong with me. I'm a screw-up. Is that it? It is, isn't it? But, wait, hang on a second—*you* made me. I know you did, and you don't make mistakes. Scripture says I am "excellently formed." Please help me remember that, and that you love me. That I'm your beloved son.

Did any of these thoughts originate with me? Clearly. But the question is, could any have originated with the Holy Spirit? The answer to that is yes as well.

And the next question is: Could any have originated with the Enemy? And the answer to that one is yes too. You see, there's condemnation here. There are messages that stand in contrast to the weight, spirit, and content of God's voice.

So let's take another look—and this time insert annotations showing our best reckoning as to the originator of each thought, based upon our *effect* analysis.

> God, I know you have good plans for me (Holy Spirit). But this life I'm leading, it doesn't feel right (me). I'm anxious so much of the time (me). I'm working so hard, but I can never seem to break through to peace and joy (me). And everyone else seems to have it all together (Enemy). No one else has any problems (Enemy). There must be something wrong with me (Enemy). I'm a screw-up (Enemy). Is that it

(me)? It is, isn't it (Enemy)? But, wait, hang on a second—you made me (Holy Spirit). I know you did, and you don't make mistakes (Holy Spirit). Scripture says I am "excellently formed" (Holy Spirit). Please help me remember that, and that you love me (Holy Spirit). That I'm your beloved son (Holy Spirit).

● ● ●

> We tend to be more skeptical of the words of others—and less so about our thoughts. We're more used to applying discernment to the former: "What he said to me, that didn't sound right" or "What she wrote, I don't agree with that." We tend to reject things said by others out of anger or frustration or out of seeming fear, prejudice, bias, insecurity, or ignorance. And we tend to accept those that sound rooted in the truth of Jesus.
>
> But we should apply the same type of skepticism, and the same level, to our own thoughts—especially when we're in prayer. As they pass through our minds, we must get used to stepping back and turning our thoughts over, asking ourselves: *Are these in alignment with biblical truth, modeled and taught to us by Jesus? Or are they not?*

And this is how we tune in. It's simply this: we listen. In prayer, actively, and with intentionality. If we hear something (or someone else does) and it fits with Scripture, if it has the unique characteristics we come to recognize, then we can trust its accuracy. And over time, we can begin to recognize what Dallas Willard calls the "unmistakable stamp of divine quality, spirit, intent, and origination."[5] Over time, we can begin to recognize the *call sign* of God.

Here's another example, a very simple one. Paul wrote, "No one can say 'Jesus is Lord' except in the Holy Spirit" (1 Cor. 12:3). What he was saying was this: no one can say, "Jesus is Lord," *and mean it,* without having his or her thoughts influenced and having it suggested to him or her by the Holy Spirit.

Look for the effect.

If you've said those words—or any like them—you've heard God's voice. You must have. That effect cannot come about any other way.

There are, undoubtedly, many thoughts that you've had that you wouldn't have had, things you've done that you wouldn't have done, without first having heard the voice of God and having had your choices—your identity—shaped by him. For example, when a thought triggered you to help a person in need; when a thought prompted you to speak up for someone who needed an advocate; when a thought moved you to have a tough, good conversation with a friend; when you felt an impulse to pray for someone who was hurting; when a friend encouraged you to confess something you didn't want to confess; when an acquaintance asked you to share your faith; when a sermon nudged you back into the Bible.

Effect.

When we open our eyes to him like this, to how he works, we men often realize we've been hearing God's voice our whole lives—we just didn't recognize it. (I didn't.) We may have just assumed these thoughts were ours—originated by us, and not by a good and almighty God.

Now, no matter how practiced we get at hearing God's voice, we'll never achieve infallibility. We must always allow for error—whether we've been trying for ten minutes or we've been doing it for ten years.

So when we hear something, when we think God's brought a thought into our minds—whether our own or whether the minds of people we know—we must remember that all human minds are fallible, and all human beings can mishear and misunderstand.

And we mustn't ever treat the things we've heard as having Scripture-level authority. They sit below Scripture, always. Scripture is the standard we know to be straight and true and authoritative. Nothing can come close to replacing it.

But once we *do* begin to recognize his voice, once we *can* recognize it, we're able to then begin our apprenticeships. Once we learn to hear the voice of our Master, we can become his *true* muckers—ready to be taught and shaped, ready for him to tell us the men we're meant to become, uniquely.

And that's the next step here—to discover how he designed us. Personally. It's for *you* to discover how he designed *you*. In the next chapter, we're going to jump right into it and learn how to ask the questions that only our Inventor can answer.

— SWITCH ON —
"MADE TO HEAR"
003

There are so many things God wants to tell you. There are so many things he wants to show you and teach you. But he needs you to learn to hear his voice. To know it. To know him.

If you want to, then keep reading. But first, take a good crack at the questions below—and do a bit of experimenting with listening prayer.

Consider these questions and jot down your responses.

003.1　　What do you think about the notion that God originates thoughts? Do you think he's ever originated them for you? When?

003.2　　Have you ever heard something from a friend, a follower of Jesus, which sounded like it might actually have been, originally, from God? When? What did you hear?

003.3　　What constitutes noise in your life right now? What's most likely to crowd God's voice?

003.4　　How noisy is your life? Does God have an opportunity to speak?

<<Enough Quiet and Solitude - - - - - - -Lots of Noise>>
　1　2　3　4　5　6　7　8　9　10

Experiment with listening prayer. Invite the Holy Spirit to direct your thoughts. Pray against distraction, against fatigue, against confusion. Then, simply ask God a single question. Maybe this: "What spiritual practice would bring me life in this season?" Or, "Is there someone with whom you'd like me to connect or reconnect?" Keep it simple.

Remain quiet for a length of time—whatever's comfortable—and listen for the inner voice. Don't try too hard. Don't overthink it. If we want to hear, if we take some time to listen in silence, we're sure to hear God at some point, in some way. He wants to speak to you.

When and if you think you might have heard something, simply test it against Scripture—invite a mature believer to comment, if you think it would be helpful. Ask: Does this fit within biblical principles? Does it bear the call sign of God? If it does, believe it. If it encourages an action, be bold and take it.

Keep good notes. As you work through the Switch On activities at the end of each chapter, make sure to collect and preserve your answers, thoughts, and the things you hear from God. It's precious data. (Also, looking ahead to the final chapter, it'll help to have it all—and have it all in one place.)

004

SPRUCE AND ALUMINUM
AND CONFIDENCE

"Father's home!"

The words shouted all through the house. The children spied him coming up the concrete walk—suitcase in hand, arms full of brown paper packages—and it triggered a happy explosion.

Outside the front door the man pauses. Hearing the commotion inside, he smiles to himself. He's so glad to be home, back in Cedar Rapids. He loves doing the Lord's work, crisscrossing the American West but hates being gone so much. He misses his family.

The man sets down his suitcase and doesn't drop a single package. The noise inside dies down. He listens … then the door bursts open. Five children pour out. Hugs and hands grabbing at gifts. Questions so fast he can't catch them all.

He distributes the largesse as best he can, making sure each package gets to the proper young recipient. Wrapping paper flies, and he assures them that, yes, he'll tell them everything they want to know about all the people and places he's visited—all he wrote about in his many letters home. All in good time.

Through the melee, his eyes meet those of his wife. She stands in the doorway, beautiful, hair parted down the middle, pulled back.

She holds a faint smile that captures something deep. But before they move to embrace, the man has one last package—this one for the two youngest boys, ages eleven and seven.

He doesn't know it now, but that gift will launch something big.

The man is Milton Wright. His two sons are Wilbur and Orville.

• • •

Milton Wright was a bishop in the Church of the United Brethren of Christ, a Protestant denomination founded during the Great Awakening. The gift he brought home that day was a toy helicopter designed by Alphonse Pénaud, a French inventor. It was made of bamboo, paper, cork, and a rubber band. And with it, Bishop Wright roused dreams of flying.

Many years later, Orville remembered:

> Our first interest ... began when we were children. Father brought home to us a small toy actuated by a rubber spring which would lift itself into the air. We built a number of copies of this toy, which flew successfully.[1]

The Wright family was tight-knit. Their home was warm, full of love. Family members encouraged and supported one another, and the children were confident. Wilbur and Orville were especially close, but they were different. Wilbur was thoughtful and steady, a voracious reader. Orville was curious and energetic, a born maker.

The Wrights moved a lot during the brothers' early years. When they were teenagers, though, they settled back in Dayton, Ohio. Wilbur finished high school, but Orville dropped out a year before graduation to start a printing business. Wilbur soon joined him. The two also opened a bicycle shop, eventually calling it the

Wright Cycle Company. Both shops prospered, and they used the profits to turn their attention back to their shared dream.

Flying.

They began to invent things most people believed impossible. Past attempts at powered flight were brought down by three problems: developing wings that would create adequate lift, finding an effective means of propulsion, and inventing an adequate method of control. Other inventors focused on the first two, but the Wrights focused on the third. Enough work had been done, they surmised, on wings and propulsion. But no one had solved the problem of control.

Before long they had designs that needed testing.

They chose a remote set of sand dunes named Kill Devil Hills on the barrier islands known as the Outer Banks on the mid-Atlantic coast. Kill Devil Hills is about four miles from the small fishing village of Kitty Hawk, North Carolina. The dunes offered privacy, steady winds, open space, and a soft place to land. Or crash.

They experimented with kites then gliders. Their designs evolved under testing, and they eventually settled on a frame of spruce covered with stretched muslin fabric.

The breakthrough came in 1902. The brothers invented three-axis control—what pilots everywhere know as pitch, roll, and yaw. *Pitch* controls the motion of an airplane around the axis that runs from one wingtip to the other, pointing the nose of an airplane up or down. *Roll* controls the motion around the axis that runs from the nose of the airplane to the tail, causing one wing to rise and the other to fall. Controlling *yaw* means controlling motion around the axis that runs vertically from the center of the top of the airplane to the bottom; that is, it involves pointing the nose of the airplane to the left or to the right.

An automobile needs only to be controlled around one axis—yaw—left and right. A bicycle, like the ones built at the Wright Cycle Company, needs to be controlled around two—yaw and roll. That's why a bicyclist, in addition to turning the front wheel, must also *lean* to make a turn. Wilbur and Orville discovered that an airplane must be controlled around all three axes. Their three-axis control remains the standard today.

After thousands of successful glides over the dunes—the longest lasting twenty-six seconds and covering a distance of 622.5 feet—and establishing that they could make controlled turns, the brothers decided to add power. On a return trip to Dayton, they tasked their bicycle shop mechanic, Charlie Taylor, to build them an engine. He made a twelve-horsepower, four-cylinder aluminum motor. The brothers mounted it on their flyer and headed back to Kill Devil Hills.

The toss of a coin days earlier resulted in Orville taking the helm first on December 17, 1903. He flew 120 feet in twelve seconds. Wilbur flew next, covering 175 feet. Orville flew again, two hundred feet. Wilbur then made the final flight of the day. Orville described it in his notebook:

> Wilbur started the fourth and last flight at just about [twelve] o'clock. The first few hundred feet were up and down, as before, but by the time three hundred feet had been covered, the machine was under much better control. The course for the next four or five hundred feet had but little undulation. However, when out about eight hundred feet the machine began pitching again, and, in one of its darts downward, struck the ground. The distance over the ground was measured to be 852 feet.[2]

The brothers flew about a quarter mile that day, averaging about ten feet off the ground. And in those moments the world changed. In the cold and salty wind and blowing sand, they had achieved the first controlled, powered, and sustained heavier-than-air human flight.

Orville, ecstatic, walked the few miles to Kitty Hawk to send this telegram to his father:

Success four flights Thursday morning all against twenty-one mile wind started from Level with engine power alone average speed through air thirty one miles longest 57 seconds XXX home Christmas.[3]

THE WRIGHT'S FIRST SUCCESSFUL FLIGHT
KILL DEVIL HILLS, NORTH CAROLINA, 1903

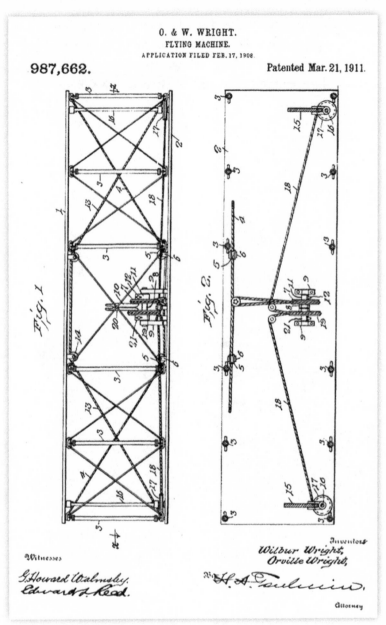

U.S. Patent No 987,662: Flying Machine

LiE:

"BECOME SOMEONE ELSE."

You've been told: *you need to prove yourself every day. You need to prove yourself to the world by fitting into its culture and competing. Conforming conceals our defects and deficiencies and allows us to make something of our lives. Here's how: we identify others who've achieved the things we want—wealth, status, power—then we do whatever they do.*

Just being you will never be enough. Become someone else. Someone better.

These are lies, and they're holding you back. **Think different.**

● ● ●

We humans are crazy complex, more mysterious and marvelous than any man-made invention.

Consider your brain. It's made up of nearly one hundred billion (100,000,000,000) neurons. These cells process information, connecting to one another by synapses, of which you have more than one hundred trillion (100,000,000,000,000). Electrical and chemical signals speed through this network, coordinating your senses, thoughts, emotions, movements. It's why you can read this—how you can process these very words.

But the wonder deepens. Every neuron, like every other cell in your body, contains an encoded description of your design. Every cell contains complete, detailed instructions for how your body is to be built and maintained—what cells need to grow and when, exactly how they must be positioned, and how they each should work and how they all should work together. *Every cell.* Every cell has a full parts list and instruction manual for building and operating the wonderfully intricate and capable you.

That's intentionality.

And it matters. God's designs matter. So when we ask Who are the men we should become? how can we not take his incredible, intricate intentionality into account? How can our questions not morph, actually, into this one: Who does our Maker *dream* we become?

"Know that the LORD, He is God; It is He who has made us, and not we ourselves" (Ps. 100:3 NKJV). Just as an aeronautical engineer would be foolish to try to understand a modern aircraft without consulting the inventor's design schematics, so too are we foolish (and reckless) when we decide whom we should become without trying to grasp the intent of the One who crafted our every cell.

So that's exactly what we're going to do in this chapter: *learn how to grasp his intent* for our lives.

Culture discourages this, of course. It trains us to look upward, but not to God. Up to other people. And we do. We start early, as boys, looking up to men and women who do amazing things on grass and turf and hardwood and ice. Heroes. As we get older, we look up to those who do amazing things in classrooms, boardrooms, laboratories, legislatures—to those who speak and create and negotiate, who research and discover and write.

Culture tells us, subtly and sometimes not so subtly, that our own designs are deficient, defective even. The designs of our heroes—those are better. So culture teaches us through its institutions to ignore our own God-given designs and simply imitate those who've gone before us, those who've become something in the world. *Man up. Become someone better.*

The thing is, God doesn't mass-produce us on some whirring and clanking assembly line—and he doesn't make mistakes. Each of us is a custom-designed, one-of-a-kind masterpiece. And God's intent for each of us is unique.

Now all this wouldn't be so bad if culture's advice was just foolish; but it's dangerous too. It's dangerous because heroic images are false images. They're incomplete, for they portray the good and obscure the bad. What we cannot see from our vantage is what's broken. And something always is: "There is no distinction: for all have sinned and fall short of the glory of God" (Rom. 3:22–23).

So when we try to model ourselves after heroic images, *we lose some of our humanity.* We lose confidence in our own God-created worth. We try to become someone else and lose our ability to be comfortable as ourselves, our *true* selves. (I did.)

But we can't ever measure up to our heroes, because they're ideals. They aren't real. They don't actually exist. We do our utmost to compete, but we're never enough. We can't possibly be.

Have you felt that? Never enough?

There's another lie at work in the world, this one contradictory. It's worth mentioning it here because some of us follow *it* instead. It's actually the opposite of "become someone else," but it's closely related and it leads to the exact same outcome. The lie is this: each of us is utterly unique (that's right), and each of us is "all good" already, perfect in every way that matters (that's not).

Just as the "become someone else" lie encourages us away from God, the "you're all good already" lie does too. Instead of trying to emulate our worldly heroes, we are the heroes.

"Become someone else" says we're not good enough. "You're all good already" says just being is good enough. It says that we don't need God. It says we don't need grace. It says we don't need to transform, further and more, into the character of Jesus. It says the men we're meant to be are simply the men we've always been.

Well, here's the truth: God's got *so* much more for us than *that* too.

•   •   •

We aren't meant to become *other* men. We're designed to be *different* men—just as an airplane's design is different from a radio's, and a radio's design is different from a light bulb's. We cannot, therefore, simply imitate other people, not when trying to answer questions this important. We're meant to become *us*, the miraculous selves God dreamed of, the men he built.

> So since we find ourselves fashioned into all these excellently formed and marvelously functioning parts in Christ's body, let's just go ahead and be what we were made to be, without enviously or pridefully comparing ourselves with each other, or trying to be something we aren't. (Rom. 12:4–6 THE MESSAGE)

To encourage inventors like the Wrights to share knowledge of their inventions, rulers and republics enact patent systems. They encourage inventors to share details of their inventions publicly for the public good. In exchange for disclosure inventors are given patents—rights, lasting for a term of years to block anyone else from making or selling the inventions they cover.

In the absence of patent systems many inventors would, no doubt, protect their inventions by instead keeping designs secret. But by offering an alternative, one that encourages public disclosure, governments can ensure that knowledge isn't lost to humanity when inventors die.

The word *patent* comes from the Latin word *patere*, which means "to lay open." The idea is that inventors lay open the inner workings of their inventions in order to obtain exclusive rights to make and sell them.

The problem is, of course, God wrote no patents. He left no patent drawings of us. Even if he did, the complexity and craftsmanship would overwhelm. We wouldn't know where to look or what to look for. How then do we lay *ourselves* open and lay hold of our Inventor's intent? How do we know with confidence what all this intricacy in our designs means?

Well we might not have patents to look at, but we have something better. We have a relationship. We have access to the Inventor himself. So what's impossible on our own—figuring out the men we're meant to become—becomes quite doable when we do it *with him*. We can find answers when we allow God to speak to us, to teach us where to look and what to look for, amid the complexity.

● ● ●

Inventions need power. A flat-panel television, a refrigerator, a wireless router—all need power, which they get in the form of electrical current from the alternating current (AC) power grid. A smartphone, a tablet, a digital camera—they get power in the form of direct current (DC) from batteries. The Wright Flyer and the bicycles built at the Wright Cycle Company got power in the form of mechanical energy, the former from the turning of an internal combustion engine, and the latter from turning of cranks by human muscles.

To do the work they're designed to do, machines need specific kinds of power.

We need specific power too. But unlike the television, the refrigerator, the smartphone, and the bicycle, we followers of Jesus are unique in that *we are able to operate on different types of power*. We can operate on our own in our own strength. Or we can operate on power from the Holy Spirit, "by the strength that God supplies" (1 Pet. 4:11).

Work we do under our own power *is* work—work that can be good, *important* even—but it's not God's work. It's not the most important and meaningful work we'll do in our lives. It's not the kind of work that'll last *beyond* our lives and into eternity. It's not the kind of work that'll give us the significance, excitement, peace, and joy that's intended for us by our Creator.

"Only the energizing of the Holy Spirit can enable the work of God," A. W. Tozer once taught. And the Holy Spirit does his energizing, explained the old preacher, "through the giving and the exercising of spiritual gifts."[4]

So when we lay ourselves open, that's what we have to look for. When we ask Who are the men we're meant to become? we must look to our unique spiritual gifts.

That's where we'll find our Maker's intent.

● ● ●

Each follower of Jesus "has received a gift," wrote the apostle Peter (1 Pet. 4:10). Note the verb. Spiritual gifts are *given*; they're not grasped for. They're given to us the moment we decide to follow Jesus, the moment we're *re*-invented. And Jesus decides who gets what. He distributes gifts by the Holy Spirit, "who apportions to each one individually as he wills" (1 Cor. 12:11). As such, our job is not to try to pick the ones we want and to reject the ones we don't. Rather, our job is to discover which ones the Holy Spirit has distributed to us already.

But what are these things?

Spiritual gifts are attributes or abilities that God energizes or empowers, and through which He works—differently, uniquely, personally—through each one of us and for the advantage of others. They enable us to do things, even supernatural things, *for other people*—and to do them in an especially effective or hearty manner and/or with uncommon frequency.

That's part of the answer. But to understand them fully, we need to understand Jesus' *purposes* in working through us in this way. To understand them fully, we need to look behind the gifts. So what are those purposes? Well, they're God's purposes. It's the grand work of the Inventor, nothing less than the redemption of our entire world.

You see, we aren't the only things being remade, being reinvented. We're just small (but key) parts of a much larger, jaw-dropping reinvention project. For when man fell so long ago in the garden of Eden, things went very wrong. Sin and rebellion entered the world. Death entered the world. Relationships broke. Everything broke.

But then after a time Jesus entered the world—and when he did, he launched God's massive project of setting things right. "God loves this created world so much," wrote Timothy Keller, that unstoppable pastor of Gotham, "that He sent his Son to redeem it … to massively and finally restore the material creation."[5]

And through our spiritual gifts, we get to be part of that epic work. And *how* we get to, that's core to our identities. For we've been designed for it, uniquely. We've been prepared.

When we make our decision to follow Jesus, we're given at least one attribute or ability to do what he does. We're given at least one attribute or ability to work in an especially effective or hearty manner and/or with uncommon frequency for the redemption and restoration of this world *by* and *through* love.

● ● ●

Spiritual gifts are not just natural talents. Though they sometimes look the same, the two are different. Everyone has natural talents, aptitudes given by God when he first made us, physically. They're connected to our physical selves. It might be that someone is well-spoken or a good leader, or that he or she is quick-witted or athletic or gregarious or street-smart or any of hundreds of other possibilities. Every person on earth has unique natural talents in various combinations and varying degrees—for every person was created by God, whether we're followers of His Son or not.

Spiritual gifts, though, are connected to our spiritual selves. They are given only to followers of Jesus, and they're given for the purpose of God's work.

Now, both our talents and gifts are important. They both provide important clues as to our design, clues as to God's intent. And they often work together.

Here's how I think about it. It's as if Jesus, through the Holy Spirit, sometimes stacks them. It's like He sometimes places spiritual gifts atop our natural talents. When He does, the spiritual gifts give the underlying natural talents *purpose* and *meaning*, which they don't have by themselves. And in return the natural talents give the spiritual gifts *context*. They give the spiritual gifts places to work in the physical world.

Here's an example: there's a man, Bill, a mentor to me. He's chairman of a Silicon Valley-based molecular diagnostics company. His leadership skills and business acumen are natural talents. God-given. But Jesus has also placed the spiritual gift of evangelism atop of his talents. The result is a man who has a formidable platform for introducing people, men and women of the marketplace, to Jesus.

When spiritual gifts are stacked on top of natural talents like this, the motivations behind our work change. Selfishness, greed, the need to prove our worth—drivers like those diminish for us. More and more, the driving force is love.

Consider another example. A talented musician. Jesus, through the Holy Spirit, could stack the spiritual gift of faith on top of this man's natural talent. The result might be someone who makes music with purpose and meaning—to bolster the faith of his fans, encouraging them to dream, to take action, to risk. His motivation in making music becomes love.

Or consider a man with a talent for building—maybe houses, maybe companies, maybe software, maybe something else. Jesus could place the gift of service on his natural talent. The result might be a man who builds with purpose and meaning—to serve others by building for them what they cannot build for themselves. His motivation in building becomes love.

Or consider a man talented in business. Jesus could stack the spiritual gift of giving on his natural talent. The result might be a man whose work running businesses is given purpose and meaning, to be successful in order to fuel his giving, monetarily, to the church, and to people in need. His motivation becomes love.

Getting a hold of our spiritual gifts and understanding how those gifts might relate to our natural talents helps us to see ourselves as God sees us. It allows us to begin to understand his intent for our lives. The way his energizing power is meant to flow through us.

What are *your* natural talents? You probably have a sense. But do you know your gifts?

● ● ●

When we men think about ourselves, we tend to think in terms of smarts, capabilities, strengths—or the lack of them. When we think about identity, we think, *I'm good at this kind of thing.* Or *I'm not good at that one.*

This is myopic. It's a mistake. But it's encouraged by the institutions of our world, and most of us have been living this way for a very long time. (I know I did.) As a result, when we make decisions about work or about our futures, we mostly base them on how we understand our natural talents. What are we good at?

But as Christian men, focusing only on this is just too narrow. Talents are *aspects* of our identities. They're not the whole thing or even the most important thing. Honestly? Focusing only on them is how we end up underutilized, insecure, and burned out.

You see, one of the major ways God blesses us over the course of our lives—with significance, excitement, peace, joy—is by allowing us to use our spiritual gifts, through the work *they* enable.

So the stakes are really high. We stand to lose so much if we're not listening for (and obedient to) what God is doing in our lives. We stand to lose so much if we're not in relationship with him. If were not being apprenticed by him.

Think how much the prophet Moses would have lost. On Mount Horeb, at the burning bush, God called Moses. He called him to bring the people of Israel out of Egypt. Moses protested, however, with talk about a lack of natural talent: "Oh, my Lord, I am not eloquent, either in the past or since you have spoken to your servant, but I am slow of speech and of tongue." God responded, "Who has made man's mouth? Who makes him mute, or deaf, or seeing, or blind? Is it not I, the LORD? Now therefore go, and I will be with your mouth and teach you what you shall speak" (Ex. 4:10–12).

Had Moses refused on account of his perceived lack of talent for speaking, he would have, presumably, continued living and working as a shepherd in Midian. But he didn't. He listened. He trusted God (after one more protest). He trusted that God had designed him to be a man who could stand up to Pharaoh, deliver his people out of slavery, and lead them. And so, he got to. He got to part the Red Sea and spend days with God on a high mountain. He got to receive manna from the sky, water from a rock, and the Ten Commandments from the Almighty.

With God, Moses' life was full, his work massive and heroic. Alone, they simply would have been much, much less.

Jesus said, "The thief comes only to steal and kill and destroy; I have come that they may have life, and have it to the full" (John 10:10 NIV).

Culture is set against us, intent on luring us into lives that are *filled* but that are far from *full*. God wants to bring abundance to you and through you. A full life.

How full is yours?

• • •

In his workshop my dad built circuit boards. They weren't the sophisticated ones he dealt with at work. He made them simple for us, built on actual wood boards. He wanted to teach my sister and me, grade-schoolers, about electricity.

Each board had three components: a battery, a switch, and something else—the part that *did* something with the power. For one, it was a light bulb. For another, a buzzer. For others, motors that did various things. So the moment of truth was the moment one of us kids hit the switch. When we did, when we applied power for the first time, that's when we got the answer to our question: What is this thing?

That was the moment of truth for Wilbur and Orville too. Once they'd completed all the experimenting they could do with kites and gliders, they did the only thing left: they applied power. They knew Charlie Taylor's engine would reveal once and for all whether the contrivance they'd built was indeed an airplane, or whether it was just a laughable dream made of spruce and muslin.

History would record, of course, at 10:35 a.m. on December 17, 1903, near Kitty Hawk, North Carolina, with Orville at the helm, that the brothers had indeed built an airplane—the world's first.

●   ●   ●

Power reveals.

It is no different for us. Power reveals *our* designs. Since our spiritual gifts are attributes and abilities to which the Holy Spirit applies power, we simply need to look back on our lives, at our experiences, our interactions with other people. We simply need to look at *what we were doing* when the Holy Spirit applied that power to us. Those are our moments of truth. In them, we'll see our spiritual gifts. We'll see our designs.

But how can we tell when the power of the Holy Spirit was with us, in us, working through us and when it wasn't? There'll be evidence, and it'll be external and internal.

Here's what the external evidence will look like: *impact.* Since spiritual gifts are directed outward, toward loving and serving other people, this is a requirement. And we learn to identify and measure impact by looking to Jesus.

At the beginning of Jesus' time of ministry, "the Holy Spirit descended on him in bodily form, like a dove" (Luke 3:21–22). Everything he did thereafter was by the power of the Holy Spirit. So Jesus is our standard. He's our model for what it looks like to work by the power of the Holy Spirit. He's our model for what it looks like to have impact.

And the internal evidence will have two parts: *inner sense* and *inner reward*. To identify the former, we employ our God-given, internal sense of discernment. As Tozer wrote, "No one ever received the Holy Spirit's power without knowing it. He always announces Himself to the inner consciousness."[6] What we look for, therefore, are instances in our pasts when we sensed the Holy Spirit on some level working through us.

To identify the latter—inner reward—we look to our hearts. We look for instances when a type of work, when we engaged in it, *brought us life* in return for our effort. It's not that the work we do in our spiritual gifts won't be hard and frustrating—at times, it'll be both, undoubtedly. It's that such work, somehow, some way, is sure to bring us significance, excitement, peace, and joy. For Jesus didn't come so we could lead aimless, boring, anxious, sorrowful lives.

Remember: *life to the full.* The work we do in our spiritual gifts is a vital and significant component of the lives he's promised.

So to answer our fundamental design question—What are our spiritual gifts?—we simply must look back on our lives and search for *moments of truth* by asking these three questions:

- When have I worked to love and serve and impact people like Jesus did?

- When have I sensed the presence and power of the Holy Spirit?

- When have I felt significance, excitement, peace, and/ or joy in work?

Whatever we were doing in those moments, when all of those line up, *those are spiritual gifts.*

Here are just a couple examples:

- If you enjoy speaking to friends who are struggling or discouraged, and lovingly admonish and/or encourage or console them; if your friends are strengthened and motivated and mature in their faith as a result; and if you sense that your words were not your own, but perhaps from the Holy Spirit, then you likely have the spiritual gift of exhortation.

- If you get satisfaction from teaching people—men, women, children—about the world and about God or about the love and truth of Jesus; if people learn from you and deepen their faith; and if you sense the energizing power of the Holy Spirit when you teach, then you likely have the spiritual gift of teaching.

● ● ●

This is essential work. "Do not neglect the gift you have," wrote the apostle Paul to his younger disciple Timothy. "Practice these things, immerse yourself in them" (1 Tim. 4:14–15).

Spiritual gifts are among the best indicators of the intentionality of our Maker. They reveal a ton about the men we're meant to become. When we bring God our questions of identity, therefore, spiritual gifts are the first thing about which we must ask. "What are mine?" That's our first fundamental question.

In the next chapter, we'll discover the second.

— SWITCH ON —
"MADE UNIQUE"
004

There is someone you're meant to become, someone you're designed to become, *someone you're going to become*. Not someone else. Just you. More you. The *true* you.

To see that man—to understand him—you must understand your spiritual gifts. So reflect on these questions below, then let's discover yours.

Consider these questions and jot down your responses.

004.1   Have you ever felt like you didn't measure up? When? How?

004.2   Have you ever tried to emulate another person for worldly reasons? Who? Why?

004.3   How would you describe your natural talents? If it's helpful, consider how others might describe them. Don't be shy. List everything that comes to mind.

Discover your spiritual gifts. Turn to appendix A. But before you go, take a minute to pray.

> *Holy Spirit my Counselor, I want to know more about myself, my true self. I want to discover my spiritual gifts. But I need your help. Your wisdom and knowledge, your ideas and inspiration—they're far beyond*

my own. I cannot gain this understanding without you.

Teach me. Speak to me. Direct my thinking as I examine each gift. As I try to quiet my mind and read and listen, let me hear your voice. Originate your thoughts in me. Come Holy Spirit. Be my guide. Amen.

005

SILVER AND MERCURY AND TRUTH

A man looks out a window in central Paris. Four stories below, residents hurry along to work, to the market. Bags, baskets, coats pulled tight. A few stop to purchase the morning papers, to get a shoeshine, but most just keep moving through the brisk morning air.

The Boulevard du Temple in the 10th Arrondissement is lined with wide sidewalks and tall trees, and it's bustling this early April morning. But when it really comes alive is at night, for it's also lined with theaters.

The man in the window knows those theaters. He's made his living in them for twenty years now, working his way up, but he's not an actor or director or writer. He's a painter. He paints scenery. Really good scenery.

The man leans against the sill and takes in the view. His mind turns. He's always looking for ways to make his paintings more realistic. Just like life is … down there.

After a few minutes, he pivots and pulls his mind back into his studio. There are canvases all over. Paints and brushes in clay and copper pots. But his eyes lock on his *camera obscura*. It sits alone on a table.

He loves that thing. He uses the simple but ingenious device all the time. It's a box with a lens at one end. Light through the lens projects an image on a screen. The image is inverted, but it's an accurate, two-dimensional rendering of whatever three-dimensional thing or scene the lens sees.

The device doesn't capture images. It just allows the man to get proportions and perspective just right—true to life—as he sketches, before the first paint stroke.

But today, for the first time, he looks at it differently. He thinks about it differently. He tilts his head, tugging gently on one end of his mustache.

"*Est-ce que ça fonctionnerait?*" ("Could it work?") To himself. Would it ever be possible to use a *camera obscura* to create images without pencils or charcoal or paint—perfect images—*permanent images?*

For the first time, the man asks, "Could a scene paint itself?"

He is Louis-Jacques-Mandé Daguerre. And he's just about to find out the answer.

● ● ●

Daguerre was born in 1787, the early days of the Industrial Revolution, the first phase. His parents lived in Cormeilles-en-Parisis, a small town ten miles outside of Paris in wooded hills. Less than two years later, though, their world turned upside down, as France plunged into revolution of a different kind—violent and political. The elder Daguerre was a clerk in the French Finance Ministry, until it was wiped out by revolutionaries. He then became a clerk for a wealthy estate.

The family survived the chaos of the French Revolution, but young Daguerre's education suffered. Schools met only intermittently during his formative years because of the massive upheaval. But when old enough he apprenticed in architecture (what his father wanted) and painting (what he wanted). After a time he went to Paris and got into theater set design (a compromise).

He found home in the bohemian city. His passions for expression and innovation were exercised to great success. He was artistic, inventive, and ambitious, adept at using light and dark and color to create clever effects and illusions on stage. His designs moved audiences and brought acclaim.

But an obsession took hold—a desire to capture perfect images, permanently. At the time, a handful of scattered inventors were experimenting with light-sensitive chemicals, dreaming of grabbing fleeting scenes right out of the air and fixing them to paper. To make what we today call a *photograph*.

If he could just find the right light-sensitive substance, Daguerre figured, he could replace the internal screen of a *camera obscura* with coated plates. Projected images, he surmised, with their light areas and dark areas, would affect the surface differently, based on how the light fell. They'd leave permanent renderings of themselves. He just needed to find the right substance.

He experimented with phosphorescent powders. They held images but only for a few hours. Then in 1826 he met Nicéphore Niépce. Niépce was also experimenting with chemistry and a *camera obscura*. With different skills and backgrounds, they complemented one another. Daguerre was an artist, expert in light and optics. Niépce, though without formal training, knew chemistry. He was self-taught but doggedly determined in practical experimentation. He read books and journals and just tried things.

Niépce had some success with bitumen of Judea, a black, tar-like substance. When he inserted a bitumen-coated plate into a *camera obscura*, the areas exposed to the light portions of a given projected image would harden; the dark portions, because they weren't exposed to as much light, wouldn't. The unhardened bitumen could then be removed with a solvent.

It was with this that Niépce captured history's first photograph: *View from the Window at Le Gras*, from an upstairs window of his estate house in eastern France. It was far from perfect, but it was still a breakthrough.

But a problem remained: bitumen had to be exposed to an image for *days*.

So the men continued to work. They experimented with chemicals, compounds, and processes, and they shared their findings. Niépce focused on bitumen. Daguerre looked for new options, believing bitumen took far too long.

People have known of the light-sensitive nature of silver salts since the thirteenth century. Unlike bitumen, such compounds *darken* rather than harden when exposed to light. Daguerre began using copper plates coated with a thin layer of polished silver "sensitized" by iodine vapors. This allowed him to capture images more distinct than Niépce's, but it still took up to eight hours for exposure.

For four years, the two men progressed by luck and stubborn trial and error. It was fruitful, their partnership, but it came to an abrupt end. Niépce died of a stroke in 1833. It was enough, though, to launch Daguerre ahead of all competitors. And he continued right on with his single-minded experimentation, focusing on narrowing his process to something that he could sell to the public.

He then—by accident—made his crucial discovery. What he didn't yet understand was that his silver iodide plates, when exposed to an image for even a few minutes, *did* capture images. The images just remained invisible and needed to be *developed*.

The story goes that he left one of his exposed plates in a chemical cupboard for a few days. When he brought it out again, he saw a surprisingly sharp picture that hadn't been there before. Investigating, he found a broken mercury thermometer in the cabinet. He began experimenting. He found that mercury vapor condenses on silver iodide but *only where it's been exposed to light*. That condensation is what was needed. The invisible became visible.

And what he saw was amazing.

EARLY PHOTOGRAPH: BOULEVARD DU TEMPLE
PARIS, FRANCE, 1838

Samuel F. B. Morse, inventor of Morse code and contributor to the inventing of the telegraph system, was the first American to see one of Daguerre's creations. He described it this way:

> The exquisite minuteness of the delineation cannot be conceived. No painting or engraving ever approached it. For example: in a view up the street a distant sign would be perceived, and the eye could just discern that there were lines of letters upon it, but so minute as not to be read with the naked eye. By the assistance of a powerful lens, which magnified fifty times, applied to the delineation, every letter was clearly and distinctly legible, and so were the minutest breaks and lines in the walls of the buildings and the pavements of the street.[1]

The scene did indeed paint itself *and with astonishing beauty and clarity.*

The year was 1839, and Louis Daguerre finally had what no one else did—a practical and commercially viable photographic process. He disclosed it to the world at The Institut de France, naming his product the "daguerreotype."

"I have seized the light. I have arrested its flight," he said.[2]

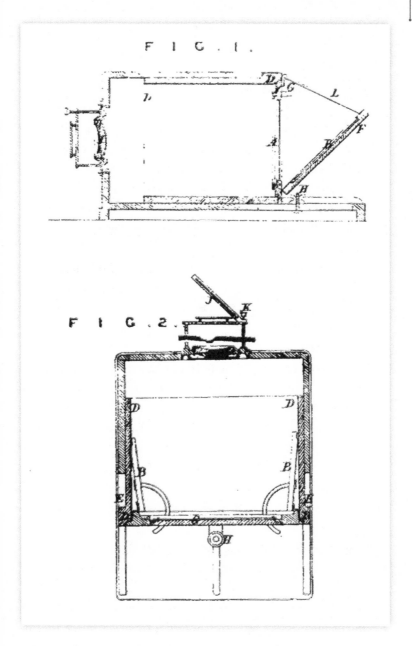

BRITISH PATENT Nº 8194: OBTAINING DAGUERREOTYPE PORTRAITS

LiE:

"MAKE A NAME FOR YOURSELF."

You've been told: *you must be known. You must be known by a great name: Strong. Smart. Successful. Rich. Connected. Loved. Respected. Stronger. Smarter. Better. But who can choose it? Well, you can. You know yourself. You know how the world works. Just make sure you choose a name that'll remove all doubt. Then go out there and earn it.*

Making a name for yourself—this is the essence of manhood.

These are lies, and they're holding you back. **Think different.**

● ● ●

We need names.

We have names given to us by our parents, of course—they're on our birth certificates and passports. But there are other kinds of names that are just as important. Maybe more so. Somewhere deep in our inner machinery, we know we need these other names— names that tell us (and everyone) not just what we're called but what we *mean*.

But too often we end up with the wrong names. And that can, literally, destroy our lives. You see, we need names—but the *right* ones.

And if we discover those, if we adopt them, if we allow God to apprentice us into them, we can enter into, much further, the full lives that God intends.

The problem is that we're just not very good at naming. It's a difficult business, at least for those not involved in the inventing process. Naming follows inventing, and we didn't do the inventing.

But we're apprenticed to the One who did. We're in relationship with the One who loves us and knows us—*all the way*. George MacDonald, the great Scot poet, wrote this:

> The true name is one which expresses the character, the nature, the being, the meaning of the person who bears it. It is the man's own symbol—his soul's picture, in a word—the sign which belongs to him and to no one else. Who can give a man this, his own name? God alone. For no one but God sees what the man is, or even, seeing what he is, could express in a name-word the sum and harmony of what he sees.[3]

What's *your* soul's picture, in a word? How does your Maker think of you? What's *your* true name?

Want to discover it?

• • •

In the mid-1800s, people connected Daguerre's invention with the brand concepts of beauty, quality, even infallibility—and they flocked to daguerreotypists. The name "daguerreotype" meant something to them.

Decisions become simple when we see a brand name that we link with positive qualities. They do for us today in our everyday purchasing lives. Names help us decide. They accomplish a lot with very little—just a word, maybe two. And they do their connecting work *efficiently*, in ways that are *tight* and *authentic*.

Imagine searching the internet for a camera and narrowing to two options similar in price. One doesn't have a brand name but has a credible and compelling product description. The description tells you the particular camera is made with high-quality materials, is durable, and is well designed. The other option is a Leica—a hundred-year-old brand connected with craftsmanship, design, and adventure. For most of us, it wouldn't be much of a choice. Names help us decide.

Companies use names to their advantage, but so do men. Something in our human framework drives us to make them for ourselves—the names we want.

We've known that drive a very long time. These are the exact words, in fact, that appear in the book of Genesis, spoken by men in arrogance and pride and insecurity, who planned to build the Tower of Babel: "Then they said, 'Come, let us build ourselves a city and a tower with its top in the heavens, and let us make a name for ourselves'" (Gen. 11:4).

We bend names to our purposes. We use them. We try to answer our deepest questions of identity by connecting ourselves to positive things, to things we believe have power. (I did that.) We make names and affix them to ourselves, pretending they are real, trying to make them real. Trying to live them out.

Strong. Smart. Successful. Rich. Connected. Loved. Respected. Stronger. Smarter. Better.

And we make this process public, subtly working to influence others to name us in the way we want. We strive by our own strength to make for ourselves the names we've decided we want or think we need, instead of seeking names from our Maker and Master, our Most High God.

But we *can* seek names from him.

We have that kind of access—to him, to his voice.

● ● ●

Human beings make several hundred to several thousand decisions per day. That's hundreds of thousands to *millions* of decisions per year—between tens of millions and hundreds of millions over a lifetime. A few are big and important, whether and who to marry, one's career, and so on. Most of them are small and carry much less weight. At least they seem to. But taken together these decisions become our lives.

So how do we make good decisions? Under ideal circumstances, we're able to investigate and inform ourselves as to whether a particular decision aligns with our beliefs, values, priorities, and identities. In the rush and charge, though, when things are happening fast—interactions with others especially—and when decisions must be made in real time, it's difficult to weigh everything.

But names help us decide. Names simplify. We can walk into any situation, and rather than weighing any complexities we can simply *be* our names.

The apostle Paul called us "holy and beloved" (Col. 3:12). If you or I were to accept and adopt the name *Beloved*, for example, we could go to work as that, we could come home to spouses and kids as that, we could interact with friends in the full knowledge of our secure position as beloved sons of God Almighty, hand-picked by him, needing validation from nothing else and no one else.

Names are powerful. With some work and determination and consistency, we can often become the things we want to become. We can earn the names we covet. Daguerre made thousands of decisions, maybe more, toward becoming "great inventor." He very much wanted that name. And he got it. He's one of only seventy-two Frenchmen to have their names engraved on the Eiffel Tower—men chosen for their contributions to science, engineering, math, and industry.

But the thing is, if we bear the *wrong* names, we live out wrong beliefs about ourselves and about God. And we make so many wrong decisions. We ignore the intentionality of our Inventor. We don't live as God intends us to live or love as he intends us to love.

If we bear the wrong names, *we live the wrong lives.*

● ● ●

Because names are efficient and effective, they're sometimes used in ways that are less than honorable. Consider FUD—an acronym for a sales tactic allegedly pioneered by IBM in the 1970s. Gene Amdahl, early tech pioneer known for work on mainframes, first at IBM and then at his own company, Amdahl Corporation, was the first to define it: "FUD is the *f*ear, *u*ncertainty, and *d*oubt that IBM salespeople instill in the minds of potential customers who might be considering [Amdahl] products."[4]

FUD focuses not on the positive aspects and benefits of one's own products but on pushing negative and often dubious information about those of competitors. And names are the primary weapons: *insufficient, unreliable, shoddy, defective, low quality, unstable, unsound, unsafe, not secure, gimmicky, outmoded, obsolete*. Because overt FUD often results in litigation, these names are bestowed covertly in jokes, whispers, offhand comments, off-the-record conversations.

We're hit with FUD too, and it's the Evil One who *really* pioneered it. His very first words in the garden of Eden were FUD. He stoked fear, created uncertainty, and fostered doubt about Adam's and Eve's identities in relation to God. And, with us, he often uses names to do it. But these are the names we don't want: *Idiot, Failure, Freak, Mistake, Unworthy, Unloved, Unlovable, Uncared-for, Forgotten*. (I've believed some of these were mine.)

These are also bestowed covertly, whispers spoken into our thoughts or, tragically, through the voices of people around us. Some cruel and intentional, others well-meaning or unthinking but no less damaging.

● ● ●

One man who understood the power of names was King Nebuchadnezzar II of Babylon. About six hundred years before Jesus was born, Nebuchadnezzar sacked Jerusalem, destroyed Solomon's temple, and took a large percentage of the Hebrew population of Judea back to Babylon, including many of its most prominent families—craftsmen, artisans, people like that. Among those taken were three men: Hannaniah, Misha'el, and Azariah.

Nebuchadnezzar immersed them in Babylonian language, literature, and food. He wanted these men to adopt his culture, to become part of it. He also wanted them to adopt his gods. So he forced them to change their names. Hannaniah became Shadrach. Misha'el became Meshach. Azariah became Abednego. Their Hebrew names honored the God of Israel. Their new names honored the gods of the Babylonians.

By changing their names, Nebuchadnezzar sought to shape Hannaniah, Misha'el, and Azariah. He wanted them to live different lives. He knew that names help us decide. He wanted them to live and make decisions in their new names rather than in their old ones.

But it didn't work.

After the king commissioned a nine-story statue made of gold, he held a dedication ceremony. The Babylonian herald commanded, "Fall down and worship the golden image" (Dan. 3:5). Whoever did not, the herald warned, "shall immediately be cast into a burning fiery furnace" (v. 6). Well Hannaniah, Misha'el, and Azariah refused and were brought before Nebuchadnezzar, who gave them a second chance. To this they replied,

> O Nebuchadnezzar, we have no need to answer you
> in this matter. If this be so, our God whom we serve
> is able to deliver us from the burning fiery furnace,
> and he will deliver us out of your hand, O king. But
> if not, be it known to you, O king, that we will not
> serve your gods or worship the golden image that
> you have set up. (vv. 16–18)

Instead of making decisions in their false names, they remembered their true ones: Hannaniah means "God who is gracious" in Hebrew, Misha'el means "Who is like God," and Azariah means "God has helped."

Nebuchadnezzar was furious. He ordered the furnace to be heated seven times its normal operating temperature—so hot the guards who pushed the three men into the furnace died when they got close. But Hannaniah, Misha'el, and Azariah didn't die, and they went all the way in. They weren't burned. They weren't harmed at all. They knew who they were. They knew their God. They made a decision based upon that knowledge, and the God they knew protected them.

Think what Hannaniah, Misha'el, and Azariah would have lost had they bowed to their Babylonian names: Shadrach meant "Aku's Command" (Aku was a moon god), Meshach meant "Who is what Aku is," and Abednego meant "Servant of Nego or Nebo" (Nebo was a god of wisdom).

But they didn't; they lived *full* lives. They did something massive and heroic, something we celebrate millennia after Nebuchadnezzer's statue crumbled.

The power of a true name.

●　●　●

New inventions need new names. And who should give them? Inventors.

Years ago my father devised a new release mechanism for ski bindings. He worked on it for years. He perfected it. He patented it. Ultimately though, the state of the art caught up and passed his work. But since he'd invented the thing, he got to name it nonetheless.

He called it … wait for it … *Ski Release*. (Because that's what you get when an engineer tries his hand at marketing.) But he could call it what he wanted, just as Daguerre could, with his daguerreotype. Inventors have naming authority.

God—and God alone—has naming authority for us. Naming follows inventing, and he's the one who formed our every atom, arranged our every molecule, and who, standing in eternity, planned our every day. As George MacDonald asked above, who else could name us? No one. Certainly not this broken world. Certainly not a culture set against us.

Now, God did delegate *some* of his naming authority, of course, allowing Adam to name the animals in the creation story and allowing parents to name their children, like Eve did for Seth (Gen. 4:25).

But God reserves for himself the deepest naming—what we might best call our *true names*. He doesn't delegate that authority.

Here's an example. God bestowed a true name on a man named Abram long after the man's birth. He told him, "I have made you the father of a multitude of nations. I will make you exceedingly fruitful, and I will make you into nations, and kings shall come from you" (17:5–6). But he didn't just *tell* him. No, God also gave him a new name. "No longer shall your name be called Abram," God said, "but your name shall be Abraham" (v. 5) In Hebrew *Abram* means "high father" or "father is exalted." But *Abraham* means "father of a multitude."

True names aren't mere designators simply for the purpose of identification. They're much more. They call us into true identity as they pull us into God's work. True names, God's names, are *operative*. They're intentionally infused with truth and depth and meaning, meant to give us simple, accurate pictures of ourselves. Pictures of what we can become if we're willing.

Here's how I imagine the subtext of this interaction between God and Abram:

> Abram, I see beyond who you are right now—nearly a century old, without any children. I see through your current circumstances to a future I dreamed up—and it's a good one. I want you to become a father of kings and of nations; I want you to become *My* Abraham. See what I see; believe it, make decisions in it, your true identity. I know you may not reflect it right now, but let's call the name

forth, you and I, with My grace, with My power, and with your obedience.

Few things give us conviction like a name. They help us decide. They help us accept who we are. They help us be and become.

You see, we can be *told* of our identities—of our spiritual gifts, for example—but we won't internalize those identities as much as when we're named according to them. It's one thing to discover the spiritual gift of teaching, for example. But it's another thing altogether to be named *Teacher* by our Maker. It's something else entirely for God to tell us we are *Teacher* to him—*that's* how he sees us; *that's* the sum and harmony of us; *that's* our soul's picture, in a word.

Or *Shepherd* or *Navigator* or *Coach* or *Clarion* or *Witness*, perhaps. Or whatever else he's devised.

We must let him do this for us.

We're in relationship with him, apprenticed to him. We hear his voice.

Listen for the whisper. He will name you.

●　●　●

Two generations after naming Abraham, God did it again. First he delivered on the promise contained in Abraham's true name by giving him descendants, then he bestowed a true name on his grandson, Jacob.

Jacob means "deceiver" and "supplanter"—and Jacob lived up to it. Into early adulthood, he was a liar and an opportunist. Famously, he tried to make for himself what he thought would be a better name—maybe *Rich, Respected, First-in-Line*—by conspiring to trick his father into giving him his older brother Esau's blessing, which would give him a superior position in the family and a larger inheritance. Rather than looking to God for his true name, Jacob tried to make a name for himself, but he only actually succeeded in living up to his original one.

Jacob fled his home to avoid Esau's anger. After two decades of self-imposed exile, God decided to give Jacob something new, for he had bigger, better, more holy plans for him:

> And Jacob was left alone. And a man wrestled with him until the breaking of the day. When the man saw that he did not prevail against Jacob, he touched his hip socket, and Jacob's hip was put out of joint as he wrestled with him. Then he said, "Let me go, for the day has broken." But Jacob said, "I will not let you go unless you bless me." And he said to him, "What is your name?" And he said, "Jacob." Then he said, "Your name shall no longer be called Jacob, but Israel, for you have striven with God and with men, and have prevailed." (Gen. 32:24–28)

God knew Jacob better than he knew himself. He knew Jacob could be something more than a liar or a cheater. He knew Jacob could be a leader, tough and determined, but humble too. So God sought to change Jacob's mind about himself. He sought to simplify things for him. He sought to help Jacob decide who he really was. Names help us decide.

God could have just *told* Jacob he wasn't a deceiver or a supplanter. He could have told him simply: "Henceforth, thou shalt be celebrated not for craft and artful management but for true valour," as paraphrased by sharp old Welsh commentator Matthew Henry.[5] But he didn't. He did something more intimate, more compelling, closer, more authentic.

He gave him a true name.

● ● ●

It gets better. Jesus bestows true names too. His did it with a man named Simon. In their very first encounter, "Jesus looked at him and

said, 'You are Simon the son of John. You shall be called Cephas'
(which means Peter)" (John 1:42). Explaining the scene, John
Ortberg, my wise and witty pastor, said this:

> Peter is from "petra," the Greek word for "rock."
> Petra. Rock. Bulldog. Nobody had ever looked at
> Peter before and seen a rock. He was unstable and
> impulsive and as up and down as a roller coaster.
> Jesus saw it. It was in him; God had put it in him.
> Jesus saw it and gave him its name.[6]

Later Jesus told Peter *why* his true name—Peter, petra, rock—
was so important: "I tell you, you are Peter, and on this rock I will
build my church, and the gates of hell shall not prevail against it"
(Matt. 16:18).

Jesus was giving Peter his soul's picture in a word, a picture he
couldn't see on his own. He was inviting him into true identity. He
was simplifying things. He was telling him, "You're a rock, Peter. Be
Peter. Decide. Don't be anyone else. *Don't live the wrong life.*"

Knowing our true names, we're able to enter situations con-
fidently, with much better knowledge of ourselves, reflecting the
intentionality of our Inventor. With conviction we can begin pulling
God's future forward by acting in ways consistent with his knowledge of us.

We can literally transform ourselves, bit by bit, into our true
selves by trying to live each day, now, in our true names ... once we
know them.

And when we do we can be sure we're living the *right* lives.

●　　●　　●

Our God today is the same God who dreamed about Abraham, carefully designed him, and spoke to him a new name. He's not changed
one bit from that day to this. He's the same God who dreamed about

Jacob, carefully designed him, and spoke to him a new name. And he's the same God who dreamed about Peter, carefully designed him, and spoke to him a new name.

Just as he wanted to speak identity into those men in their day, he wants to speak identity into you and me today.

Do you want to know your true name? Do you want to ask God for it?

This is the second fundamental question we need to ask in our search for identity, and it'll be most useful as we get into what's coming up next—calling.

— SWITCH ON —
"GOD NAMED"
005

God, your Maker, has a name for you. His name. Your soul's picture in a word. And knowing it will help you understand even more about the man you're meant to become.

So ponder the questions below, capture your answers, then let's see what God is ready to reveal.

Consider these questions and jot down your responses.

005.1   Have you ever worked to make a name for yourself? Why? What motivated you?

005.2   What names have you tried to make? Create an honest list. Examine each phase of your life: childhood, young-adulthood, and adulthood. Include everything you can.

005.3   What questions were you trying to answer with the names on your list? What doubts about yourself were you trying to overcome?

Experiment with listening for a true name.* Let God teach you, guide you. Bestselling author and salty sage John Eldredge offered

---

*Whether these names are the secret names referenced in Revelation 2:17, I don't know. There are some writers who say they are; others who say they're not. What I do know is that the work of seeking identity is full of mystery. And what I do believe is that God will answer our questions when we ask him in his own way and in his own time (as he promises in Matt. 7:7–8). Just as I believe that he'll reveal our spiritual gifts and our callings if we ask, I believe he'll tell us what he thinks of us—who we are to him. I believe he will tell us our true names.

this wisdom: "There is no formula. You go into the wilderness with God. Ask: What do I mean to you? Who am I, to you? Tell me what you think of me?"[7] It's just that simple. Some men pray in solitude, asking these kinds of questions and listening for God's still small voice. Some men pray with other men, acting as intermediaries for one another.

When we engage God in this way—however we do it—he's sure to answer at some point in some way, probably in one we won't expect. Maybe he'll highlight a character from literature or film or even Scripture, or maybe he'll speak to us descriptive names like *Medic*, *Liberator*, *Pathfinder*, *Mighty Oak*, *Mason*. God can be as creative and inventive as he wants to be. Just make sure to test everything against Scripture and trust the insights of friends, mature believers.

And if you struggle to hear, don't sweat it. Don't dwell on it. Just try again later. Move on to the next chapter. Keep moving. Keep reading. Then come back and ask again. Listen again.

And if you feel like it, you can—in the meantime—go right ahead and adopt one of these names: *Light* (Matt. 5:14), *Conqueror* (Rom. 8:37), *New Creation* (2 Cor. 5:17), *Free* (Gal. 5:1), or *Chosen* (Col. 3:12). For these names apply to *every one of us*. And they're as true as anything else. So if you want to, just choose the one that speaks to your heart, and begin to wear it with confidence.

Pray about your names.

> *God my Father, Jesus my King, I confess I've wanted to make a name for myself. I did it because I've believed things about myself that just aren't true. I tried on my own to overcome self-doubt and prove my worth to the world.*
>
> *Right now I repent of my wrong beliefs. I choose to think differently. I turn my back on doubt. I turn my back on the names I tried to create. I want to break the power they've held on my life. I renounce them, and I resolve to make decisions in them no more.*

Thank you for revealing what's true. Thank you for giving me a picture of my true identity. Thank you for revealing to me a true name. From today forward I resolve to make decisions in that name instead. I declare that I am that man. That name. I declare that I am your man. Your beloved son. Amen.

006

COPPER AND ACID AND SIGNIFICANCE

A boy of sixteen makes his way through cold streets and a gathering mist, between buildings, down narrow alleys, then skirting the gardens of Edinburgh Castle. He is tall and purposeful, cutting across the wet grass, striding across a wide boulevard over to South Charlotte Street, then up the steps at No. 13. He unlocks the heavy black door, stomps his feet, steps in, and begins up the stairs. But before he reaches the second floor landing he already hears voices and laughter above.

It's "Hogmanay"—New Year's Eve. Family and friends have been arriving all afternoon. His family owns the four-story townhouse, but lives only on the two topmost floors, renting out the bottom. Their floors are divided into ten rooms—more than enough for a family of five. But as the boy steps into the warm glow of home and holiday cheer, the rooms feel full, filled with love and loved ones who've come for the celebration.

He greets his aunt with a hug, his uncle with a handshake, and his cousins—and a bunch of longtime family friends—with warm hellos. He makes small talk, updates them on his new pupil/teacher position at Weston House Academy.

He jokes with his brothers, Melville (Melly) and Edward, and does voice tricks for the younger revelers. His tricks are well-known and well-loved. He imitates animals with astonishing precision. And with a little encouragement, he does this thing where he runs around pretending to chase a buzzing bumblebee, catching it in his hands and letting it go again. His sounds are so realistic that the kids are fooled every time.

After a while, his father calls dinner. All file into the dining room and find a place around the dining table. The boy makes sure, as always, to sit right beside his mother. The table before them is piled high. Soup, haggis, steak pies, and "rumbledethumps." Mouth watering, the boy also spies cranachan for dessert.

A prayer of thanks and a blessing of the food prove the calm before the storm. When his father finishes, conversation erupts. Plates clink. Dishes are passed around. But throughout the joyous noise, the boy fingerspells under the table. He uses sign language, discreetly, to keep his mother apprised of everything that's being said in real time. He doesn't want her to miss a thing.

"FATHER AGAIN TALK ABOUT WORK."

"MELLY DISCUSS MEET FRIEND UNIVERSITY."

That boy, so caring toward his mother, is Alexander Graham Bell, and his heart will change how we *all* stay connected.

● ● ●

Bell's family was preoccupied with sound and speech. His father, Alexander Melville Bell, was a professor of elocution. His grandfather was an expert in phonetics. But his mother, Eliza, was deaf.

His father's influence fostered a unique appreciation for sound. The younger Bell could, from his bed, pick out specific church bells as they pealed through the darkness of the Scottish city of Edinburgh.

But his mother couldn't share in the sounds he'd grown to love—and it actually kept them close. He worked hard, even as a youngster, to keep her connected to the world. He learned sign language for public situations. And in private ones, he'd speak close to her forehead so she could sense the deep vibrations of his voice.

He was also close with his two brothers—one older, one younger. When the two oldest were in their mid-teens, their father offered them a test: build a speaking automaton. They rose to his unconventional challenge. They studied skulls. They studied gums, hard palates, teeth, tongues, lips, and larynxes. They scavenged materials: wood, rubber, metal.

And the boys did it.

Their mechanical head could say "Mama" when they blew air through its artificial windpipe and moved its mouth. It was good enough to pull a good prank on a neighbor, imitating a bawling baby.

Growing up Bell caught the invention bug. He had a strong, curious mind and shared the family obsession. It didn't take long before he began to wonder if he could send speech by electronic means. For if he could—if he could send a *human voice* across a wire, rather than merely the electronic impulses of Morse's dots and dashes—communication would never be the same.

Bell began to dream and experiment. He also worked on and off as a teacher for children who were deaf and took university classes. But in the evenings he threw himself into study, experimenting with acoustics and electricity, until dawn overtook the lamplight.

In the midst of this, though, sorrow and dislocation visited. Within a short time, both of Bell's brothers died from complications from tuberculosis. And fearing they might lose their remaining son, Bell's parents left Europe for the healthier climate of Canada.

Once settled in Ontario, though thousands of miles from everything familiar, it didn't take long for Bell to return to his experiments. But he needed money too. So when his father declined an offer to teach in Boston (at what today is the Horace Mann School for the Deaf), he suggested Bell for the position. They offered. He accepted.

One student he met was Helen Keller. Keller had come to the school as a little girl who was deaf, blind, and unable to speak, and she loved Bell right away. About their first meeting she said: "I did not dream that interview would be the door through which I should pass from darkness into light, from isolation to friendship, companionship, knowledge, love."[1]

BELL AT THE PEMBERTON AVE. (LATER HORACE MANN) SCHOOL
FOR THE DEAF (AT THE TOP OF THE STAIRS, ON THE RIGHT)
BOSTON, MASSACHUSETTS, 1871

Boston was good for Bell. The city was becoming an epicenter of technological innovation and discovery. But as he tended to do, he got busy. Very busy. In addition to teaching, he began tutoring. Then in 1873 he became a professor at Boston University.

As a teacher and tutor, Bell was professional; but as an inventor, he was dogged. For when not teaching or tutoring, he withdrew to his rented rooms-turned-workshop and focused solely on his experiments.

And soon Bell's quest to transmit speech by wire became a race. Though not yet able to transmit clear speech, a formidable man named Elisha Gray had, by early 1874, transmitted music. Gray was a co-founder of the Western Electric Company, an expert in electricity—something Bell was not. But Bell was an expert in sound, and especially how humans produced and heard it—something Gray was not. So the race was on, and history awaited the winner.

In the summer of 1874, Bell made a critical breakthrough. It occurred to him that sound waves travel through air the same way electrical currents flow through conductors, like wires. He surmised, therefore, that he could build a transmitter to convert sound waves into electrical current and a receiver to convert current back into sound.

Soon thereafter, Bell had another breakthrough. He met Thomas Watson. Watson was a practical man, an engineer and designer, who could build almost anything Bell theorized and described. Bell needed Watson, and Watson liked Bell. He liked Bell's "buzzing ideas."[2]

Their work began to culminate when Bell, through a device in one of his rooms, heard Watson fiddling with the spring in a device in another. The acoustic vibrations created just the kind of sound-shaped electrical current Bell had dreamed about and hoped for. The men worked excitedly until midnight. "Before we parted," recalled Watson, "Bell sketched for me the first electric speaking telephone, beseeching me to do my utmost to have it ready to try the next morning."[3] Watson did—and it did transmit sound—though still not clear speech.

Growing impatient, though, and in one of the most opportune moves in history, one of Bell's financial backers (and his future father-in-law) took some initiative and instructed Bell's lawyer to file for a patent with the US Patent Office on Bell's behalf. The patent described what Watson had built.

In an amazing coincidence, later that very same morning, Elisha Gray too made a filing with the Patent Office. He filed a caveat. A caveat was a notice to other inventors that a particular inventor was working on a particular invention. Once filed, subsequent filings for similar inventions had to be examined before patents could be granted in order to make careful determination of who had invented first. Gray's caveat described an invention like Bell's.

But since Bell's patent was not a subsequent filing—by a matter of minutes—and because Bell could produce evidence he was first to invent, Bell won the race to invent the telephone.* Gray abandoned his caveat and didn't contest Bell's priority. And on March 7, 1876, the United States government issued patent 174,465. But that wasn't the end. For while he had his patent, he hadn't yet transmitted clear speech. That would take another three days.

Then, on the evening of March 10, 1876, Bell spoke his famous words: "Mr. Watson, come here, I want you!"[4] And when Watson heard them through a device in another room, Bell's voice was clear ... *finally*. The men cried out with excitement and joy and relief. They'd done what most thought impossible. And they repeated it again and again, their voices carrying through the wires.

A miracle the world would soon embrace ... and then take for granted.

---

*In the years that have followed, there's been much confusion and controversy about the timing and circumstances of Bell's patent filings. He was (and still is by some) accused of stealing Gray's designs. There have been more than six hundred court challenges to patent No. 174,465—and all have been decided in Bell's favor.

A. G. BELL.
TELEGRAPHY.

No. 174,465.   Patented March 7, 1876.

Fig 6.

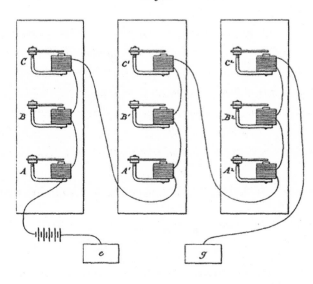

Fig. 7

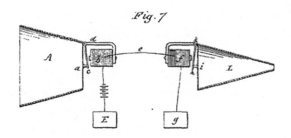

Witnesses   Inventor:

Ewelletsick).   a. Graham Bell
W. J. Hutchinson   by atty Pollok & Bailey

U.S. PATENT Nº 174,465: TELEGRAPHY

LiE:

"LOOK OUT FOR YOU."

You've been told: *you'll be happier, more fulfilled, if you focus on what you want out of life. You barely have enough bandwidth now—and you have to keep up. You can't be worrying about other people. And even if you did, wouldn't it make sense to get everything in your own life just right first? Then sometime when you have some time or extra money you'll be in an even better position to help.*

Here it is: look out for you, and everything else will work itself out.

These are lies, and they're holding you back. **Think different.**

•   •   •

This look-out-for-number-one attitude permeates our culture. It drives behavior, though we don't talk about it much. At least we don't talk about it explicitly. It's encoded into relationships, values, media, and institutions. So we learn it instead by example. By watching. Parents, peers, people we look up to.

This self-serving attitude powers our economy too, and it's done so for some time. The idea that businesses might profit by encouraging look-out-for-number-one clicked on like a light bulb in the latter part of the nineteenth century. There began to be loads of new products and lots of new consumers. And new technologies emerged too, ones that enabled companies to reach them all: inexpensive paper-making; big, fast, steam-powered printing presses.

Competition intensified, so advertisers refined tactics. The commercial version of look-out-for-number-one proved potent. It began to form the primary script of advertising: you have needs, satisfy them, expand them, demand more; that's how you'll find happiness and fulfillment. Everyone else is.

The Bell Telephone companies and their many affiliates used it in print ads to sell 600,000 phones by the turn of the century, 2.2 million by 1905, and 5.8 million by 1910. One advertisement stated this: "To be modern is to have a Bell Telephone. To have a telephone is to *live*." Another, this: "Few things give you so much convenience, happiness, and security—all rolled into one—as your telephone."

Companies today still use the commercial look-out-for-number-one. Sure their modern versions are new and improved (and more subtle), but underneath, it's the very same message.

And while it sounds appealing and seems to make some intuitive sense, it's actually dead wrong. And dangerous.

It's dangerous because it's just one more thing—one more lie—that can get in the way of us discovering the men we're made to be and the things we're meant to do. And of course, it's designed to do just that. It's specifically designed to get us doing either the *wrong work* or the right work but for the *wrong reasons*.

Think about your professional life. Over the years, how many decisions have been motivated by the drive to keep up, to prove yourself, to accumulate wealth and comfort, to build financial security?

For most of us, a lot have. (A lot sure have for me.) For we've become convinced that money and attainment are what'll bring significance and excitement, peace and joy. We've been persuaded that they'll bring "the good life."

Well, we've been duped. They won't. They never could. They'll leave us frustrated, bored, and burned out. That's the bad news.

But here's the good news: one thing that will bring significance, excitement, peace, and joy in quantities overflowing is doing what we're meant to do, the work we're designed to do, by our Maker. This work is bigger than a job, will last longer than a career, and will have more impact than anything you're likely to put on your resume. This work is the love of God applied through you to a world that needs it. And it looks different for each of us.

So what's that work for you? It's your time to turn and ask.

You ready?

● ● ●

"The inventor is a man who looks upon the world and is not contented with things as they are. He wants to improve whatever he sees, he wants to benefit the world."[5]

Alexander Graham Bell spoke those words in 1891. He was right, of course. Inventors invent with purpose. They invent for impact. Positive impact on the world, on other people.

In Genesis 2:7, when God created the first man, the Hebrew verb used to describe the creation action is *yatsar*, which translates as "to form" or "to fashion," like a potter forms clay. That word, *yatsar,* is important. It implies purpose. For a potter, like an inventor, creates with purpose *for his or her creations*. A potter forms a cup *for drinking* or a plate *for eating*. The impact is preordained by the potter. He or she forms to benefit the world *through the creation*.

Our impact—yours and mine—is preordained by our Creator God. "For we are his workmanship, created in Christ Jesus for good works, which God prepared beforehand, that we should walk in them" (Eph. 2:10). He creates us with purpose. He's made us to do specific things he can benefit the world through us. He creates us so that *we* can have positive impact on other people.

That's our nature. It isn't to look out for number one. It's to use our greatest gifts for the greatest good, for the glory of God.

So we honor the intent of our Maker, we fulfill his purposes and ours. We benefit the world *by our work*.

That's our calling.

It's a gift to us and a gift to the world. And it's what we're going to learn in this chapter.

> We don't work to earn God's love, of course. Nor do we work to earn our worth. We have God's love, and we have our worth—no matter what.
> We work because God designed us for it.

Let's break this down a bit. What do we mean by "calling"?

Well, when we decide to follow Jesus, we're called to a few things, all at once.

We're called into *relationship*—into a prayer conversation with God, into study, into praise and worship and celebration. We're called into *transformation*—into a process by which we're apprenticed more and more into the character of Jesus, and more and more into our true selves. We're called into *life*—into a different and larger kind of life, one where we begin to see and enjoy gifts from God, and where we allow ourselves to be loved by him.

But we're also called into *impact*. The call to impact is focused outward. And it's practical. It's the call to take our faith and gratitude, and mold them into action. It's the call to look beyond *number one,* and to take everything we have—our personalities, our experiences, our gifts, our interests, our passions—and turn them outward for the sake of other people.

The call to impact directs us to certain actions for certain people in certain places. As opposed to focusing on the men we're meant *to be* (spiritual gifts, true names), the call to impact is focused on the things we're meant *to do*.

This idea—what we're meant to do—is what we typically refer to as simply "calling." It's the practical *how* of following Jesus out into the world for each of us, uniquely.

It's the call to work.

But hold on … *what* work, exactly?

When asked what's most important in life, Jesus responded, "You shall love the Lord your God with all your heart and with all your soul and with all your mind" and "You shall love your neighbor as yourself" (Matt. 22:37, 39).

These are his must-do instructions. And because there are two, we can derive two functions: a primary and a secondary.

Our primary function is to respond to God's first and greatest commandment—to respond to his call to love him with everything we have. It's to respond to his call into relationship, transformation, and life. Our secondary function, though, is to respond to God's second commandment—that is, to love others. It is to respond to God's call to impact, to look out for others because he looks out for us.

We mustn't forget that we aren't the only things being reinvented. There's something much larger going on. God's also remaking and redeeming the entire world. His massive reinvention project is already underway, and now we get to join in.

We're part of what's already been remade. *We are the work.* "You are God's field, God's building" (1 Cor. 3:9). But now, having been remade, *we're also called to do our parts in the work that remains.* We're now also "God's fellow workers" (v. 9).

N. T. Wright, in his warm and deep-witted way, put it this way:

> When God saves people in this life, by working through His Spirit to bring them to faith and by leading them to follow Jesus in discipleship, prayer, holiness, hope, and love, such people are designed—it isn't too strong a word—to be a sign and foretaste of what God wants to do for the entire cosmos. What's more, such people are not just to be a sign and foretaste of the ultimate salvation; they are to be part of the means by which God makes this happen in both the present and the future.[6]

The work to which we're called—no matter how simple it seems on the surface—is nothing less than rebuilding the world. It's epic. Eternal. Jesus began it, and we're called to do our parts in pushing it forward. It's a continuation of the gospel story, a story now not just about God and Jesus and the Holy Spirit, Peter and Paul, Matthew and John, Barnabas and Apollos, Priscilla and Aquila, but about you and about me too.

But what does this work look like, practically?

For starters, it looks just like it did for Jesus: loving and serving other people—never ourselves alone—by the power of the Holy Spirit and for God's eternal purpose of reinventing and redeeming every part of this world.

It's the work of setting *everything* right—everything that's gone wrong in the world. Every hurt. Every injustice. Every mistake. Every sin. Every broken heart. Every broken life. Redeemed. Completely. Forever.

Now *that's* work worth doing. That's work worth dying for.

●   ●   ●

Callings are different from obligations. Obligations are connected to our physical selves and, for the most part, we choose them. We take on obligations to children when we choose to become parents. We take on obligations to love and serve and honor spouses when we choose marriage. We take on obligations to certain people when we choose to become friends.

Callings, by contrast, are connected to our reinvented selves, to our spiritual selves, and we don't choose them. We choose to follow Jesus, of course, but we don't choose our callings. We don't choose our unique parts in the remaking and redemption of this world. God alone gives out these assignments. And just like our spiritual gifts, which we receive upon our decision to follow Jesus, we're called into God's work upon those decisions too.

Consider the apostle Paul. He began following Jesus on the Damascus Road. Afterward, in the city of Damascus, God revealed to Paul that as a result of his decision to follow Jesus, he'd been called into epic and eternal work in a very unique and personal (and unexpected) way.

●   ●   ●

Between the ages of about eight and twelve, I'd try to spend a few hours every so often all by myself in my dad's workshop. Alone among the tools and instruments, it seemed like there was all the potential in the world. I'd cook up some plans—half-baked, but that was the point back then. I needed to experiment and learn.

I'd grab some parts, some electronic and mechanical odds and ends, some tools, a pair of safety glasses. I'd hop up on a leather stool and roll it up tight. I'd plug in the soldering iron, flip the switch, and go to work.

There'd be smoke, some sparks. A singed finger or two. And after a time, something would emerge from the curling rosin fumes and fluorescence—something a bit uncomely, uncouth, a kid version of a grown-up idea.

But if I ever got too stuck on a problem, I always knew where to go ... to the guy with the PhD.

"Hey, Dad, can you come here?"

He always did. He wouldn't build it for me; he'd show me how. He'd teach me. Guide me.

He always knew whatever I didn't.

● ● ●

The magnitude of the work of reinventing and redeeming this world is staggering. Of all the potential places, how could we possibly figure out ours? Of all the potential parts, how could we ever discover the one meant for us?

Well, God knows.

He made the world and us. He knows and loves every part of this world, just as he knows and loves every part of us. He knows *everything*. He sees *everything*. And he designs each of us to fit into certain places and to have certain impacts there. But only he knows where, and only he knows how.

So when we try to figure out our *wheres* and *hows* on our own, we risk and reach wrong conclusions.

But God never misunderstands us, and he never misunderstands the world. There's nothing he doesn't understand about our designs, about who we are and how we're meant to work. And there's nothing he doesn't understand about the world, what it needs and how it needs us.

C. S. Lewis, with his meticulous and marvelous mind, wrote this: "Creatures are not thus separate from their Creator, nor can He misunderstand them. The place for which He designs them in His scheme of things is the place they are made for."[7]

God knows us. He sees many things that we don't. We cannot know ourselves, therefore, *without him*. We cannot, no matter how hard we try.

But the good news is, we don't have to know. We're not alone here, remember? We're apprenticed to a loving master. We can hear his voice. We can ask him the *wheres* and *hows* … and we must.

Imagine for a moment a young Paul wondering these questions:

"Am I doing the right things with my life?"

"Am I doing the work I'm meant to be doing?"

"How can I find more significance and excitement
and peace and joy?"

After an encounter with the risen Jesus, the man would spend his life for others by walking something like ten thousand miles across mountains and through deserts. He'd cover maybe half that mileage again by sea, all while founding churches, writing letters, and proclaiming the message of Jesus.

Could he have known he was meant for all that without God's help, without hearing his voice?

Not … a … chance.

We face the very same odds.

● ● ●

Still the lies are strong, and our old tendencies run deep. So most of us try to live like we know more than our Maker nonetheless. We try, again and again, to live as our own masters. (I did.) We go it alone. We convince ourselves we know enough—enough about ourselves, enough about where we should fit in the world. We try to live self-made. We take what little knowledge we do have, overestimate it, and make momentous life decisions.

Scripture tells us to "work heartily, as for the Lord and not for men" (Col. 3:23). Our culture encourages just the opposite. It encourages us to work for ourselves, always putting "number one" first. It encourages us to hoard for ourselves and our immediate families the things we've been given. It encourages us into selfishness and greed and fear.

When we choose this, though, we suffer. In the absence of our good work, the world suffers too.

We violate our nature. We dishonor our designs. We become like machines designed for one kind of work, trying to do a completely different kind. It's as if Alexander Graham Bell took one of his brand new telephones and plugged it into the old telegraph system and expected it to work properly. It wouldn't have.

No wonder so many of us are anxious, angry, depressed, empty *right now*.

●　●　●

God allows hard things to happen of course. He allows tough times. They shape identity. They forge maturity. But he doesn't intend for us to be constantly unsure of ourselves, merely surviving, tired, underutilized, or isolated. He doesn't intend for us to be chronically sad or lonely or full of worry. So we don't need to be.

Because here's the holy paradox: in God's upside-down economy, the more we give away, the more we get. The more we're able to find our places and do our parts in God's plans, the more we thrive, the more we find significance and excitement, peace, and joy.

Our callings benefit other people. They allow us to impact and improve the world, but they're for us too. And they're tremendous gifts. When we begin to devote our lives to them, we begin to lead lives that are full and healthy, not narrow and empty. God's designed it this way. But we need to let him speak, to guide us, to apprentice us into them.

Jesus said his "food," his life nourishment, his fuel as a man, was "to do the will of him who sent me and to accomplish his work" (John 4:34).

That can—and should—be our source of life nourishment, *our fuel*, too.

● ● ●

Alexander Graham Bell wanted to improve the lives of people facing deafness. Helen Keller described Bell's life as one committed to breaking through the "inhuman silence which separates and estranges."[8]

His devotion was clear in both his teaching and his inventing. His work on the telephone would, in fact, pave the way for others to invent the first hearing aid. Bell described it this way:

> I had made up my mind to find that for which I was searching even if it required the remainder of my life. After innumerable failures I finally uncovered the principle for which I was searching, and I was astounded at its simplicity. I was still more astounded to discover the principle I had revealed not only beneficial in the construction of a mechanical hearing aid but it served as well as means of sending the sound of the voice over a wire.[9]

Later, after the launch of the telephone, when the public was just beginning to grapple with the magnitude of the device's potential, Bell wrote to his wife: "Of one thing I become more sure every day—that my interest in the Deaf is going to be a life-long thing with me. I see so much to be done—and so few to do it."[10]

An incredible impulse to innovate and invent drove Bell. But another one, even more powerful, lay beneath it: a desire to *look out for others.*

But why? What was behind this altruistic impulse?

Modern brain science has some thoughts. Using electromagnets and radio waves, neuroscientists can watch in real time neurons and synapses in certain areas of our brains light up and drive acts of compassion and generosity. And they can watch other areas light up and drive acts of indifference and greed or self-protection. We're capable of all of it. We get to choose every day *what we work for.*

But we function better when we work with sufficient selflessness. Our inner machinery just operates better.

There's a long-established scientific link between altruism and well-being. Being good to others, helping people, giving of our time or our money—these things boost production of neurotransmitters like dopamine, oxytocin, and endorphins. These boosts serve to increase our vibrancy and feelings of peace, satisfaction, and contentment. They also reduce anxiety, stress, and gloom—and the things that come with them, like chronic disease and death.

Altruism makes our inner machinery *hum.*

It shouldn't come as a surprise, of course. Jesus teaches us just that: "It is more blessed to give than to receive" (Acts 20:35). Eugene Peterson in *The Message* translated Jesus' words this way: "You're far happier giving than getting" (v. 35).

Working in our callings also nourishes us, fuels us, by allowing us to find *significance* ... real significance, finally. God wired us with a hunger for it, and he fulfills that hunger by matching us with significant work. It's all meant to fit, like the pieces of one of Bell's and Watson's carefully crafted devices.

But when we go looking to the world for significance—building careers, businesses, bank accounts, houses, and second houses—things don't fit so well. How could they? The significance for which we hunger is much bigger than what those can deliver.

For what could be more significant than God's work? What could matter more than the rebuilding of this world and the establishment of God's eternal kingdom?

The work of our callings doesn't just include *religious* work. To engage in it doesn't require that we become monks or ministers or pastors or priests. This is a massive undertaking Jesus has got going, and there's much to do. And all of it will be accomplished by three things: the power of God and the minds and muscles of men and women. Just about every type of work is needed, therefore, and can contribute in a unique and important way—*if it's done for God's epic, eternal purpose.*

"It is not what a man does that determines whether his work is sacred or secular," wrote A. W. Tozer, "it is why he does it."[11] Seemingly secular work can become sacred when done for God and to love and serve other people. Conversely, seemingly religious work is done in vain if it's done in selfishness or greed.

Working in our callings excites us too. And that's also fuel for the soul.

We were not designed to drag ourselves through bland, boring lives, but to live lives of adventure. Think of Jesus' Great Commission: "Go therefore and make disciples of all nations" (Matt. 28:19); "Go into all the world and proclaim the gospel to the whole creation" (Mark 16:15); "to the end of the earth" (Acts 1:8). God's designed us to work hard and take big risks for holy purposes.

My friend, Joe, works in private equity in Silicon Valley. He buys and sells stakes in companies. He's done it for years; he does it well. But that's not all. Joe and his amazing wife, Catherine, give a ton of time and money to world-rebuilding causes. Joe's work fuels their giving. They give recreationally, recklessly even—sometimes to the very edge of what's prudent for their family and sometimes beyond.

They trust God. And they live lives of significance and excitement. Every call, every email, every meeting, every trip Joe takes has greater purpose and meaning because it's directed toward something epic and eternal.

Two other married friends, Nichole and Josh, operate a steel company. Their steel gives backbone to buildings all over the San Francisco Bay area. They're talented managers and smart business people. But they, too, direct their work toward something epic and eternal. The men they employ in their steel shop are just out of prison or addiction recovery. Nichole and Josh provide help and hope to men who have very little, men who have nowhere else to turn. They love and serve these guys. They mentor them and demonstrate God's love, and they receive so much in return.

Just like Catherine and Joe, Nichole and Josh live lives of significance and excitement. Everything they do at work, no matter how menial, has purpose and meaning because of its connection to how they have been made and how they have been called.

Just like these couples, we must recast how we see work. As followers of Jesus, we're not who we were before. We've been remade. We've been reinvented. We've been repurposed. We've been given purposes bigger, better, and holier than any we had before.

We're called into a new way of living ... and *a new way of working*. While we used to work to serve ourselves, we're now free to devote ourselves to things more significant and more exciting: loving and serving other people, *even if we're doing the exact same work we were doing before*.

● ● ●

Working in our callings also fuels us by allowing us to find *peace* and *joy*.

For when we accept the ideas that we're designed uniquely and that there's work meant just for us and no others, we're freed from envy and worry about competition and comparison. We can be quite happy about the talents and gifts and successes of others. We can celebrate them honestly, because we have our own unique places in the world and our own unique work to do there.

The work of others is not ours, and ours is not theirs.

We're competitive with no one else. No one else's work can threaten or diminish our work (or our worth). We can take a deep breath, finally, and enjoy our lives—just as God wants us to.

Of course this doesn't mean we don't face urgency. We do. Because all of this also means that there are real, specific people in real, specific places whom *we* are to love, serve, help, befriend; whom *we* are to rescue from the corruption and decay of those parts of the world that are yet to be rebuilt.

There are real, specific people out there with faces and names who need you; there are people out there who need me. Working to impact those people is what is ours to do and no one else's.

So we cannot fail. And we cannot wait. It's now time to ask this, our third fundamental question of identity: What work am I made and meant for? What's my calling?

If you're ready to hear the answer, do the exercises below.

Then in the next chapter—*because life's not all about work*—we'll learn the fourth fundamental question. We'll learn how to ask God about rest and restoration, recreation and refreshment.

— SWITCH ON —
"MADE TO WORK"
006

Y ou've been called. There's work you're meant to do. And your outrageously loving Father, your mighty Maker, wants to reveal it to you and apprentice you into it.

It's vital work. You're needed. So engage with the questions below, and then let's discover as much as we can about exactly what that work is.

Consider these questions and jot down your responses.

006.1　What drives your decisions about work and money? Where would you put yourself on this spectrum? Again, brutal honesty.

<< LOOK-OUT-FOR-NUMBER-ONE - -LOOK-OUT-FOR-OTHERS>>
1　2　3　4　5　6　7　8　9　10

006.2　Have you experienced the emptiness or unexpected or unintended consequences that come with the *look-out-for-number-one* attitude? Describe how.

006.3　How do you feel, currently, in your day-to-day work?

<< DISCONTENTED, MAYBE WRONG FIT - CONTENTED, GOOD FIT >>
1　2　3　4　5　6　7　8　9　10

006.4   Have you experienced the "fuel" that comes from selflessness, from helping someone in need, from being kind when you didn't need to be, from giving of your time or money to a worthy cause? Describe what you did and how it felt.

Discover your calling. Turn to appendix B and work through the calling funnel. Before you go, though, take a minute to pray.

Holy Spirit my Counselor, again I need your help. I want to go deeper into identity. I want to know more about myself—my true self. I want to understand the calling you've put on my life. But I need your wisdom and knowledge, your ideas and inspiration. I cannot do this alone.

So speak to me. Teach me. As I examine myself, help me see what you see. Come Holy Spirit. Come and be my guide. Amen.

007

GREASE AND GASOLINE
AND RESTORATION

"*Gute Nacht*, Max. *Gute Nacht*, Friedrich."

"*Es war ein guter Tag heute. Wir sehen uns morgen früh!*" ("It was a good day today. See you in the morning!")

"*Ja. Ich seh dich morgen früh, Karl!*" ("Yes. See you tomorrow, Karl!")

The man rolls his heavy Veloziped over the shop floor, toward the garage doors.

He stops just outside under the painted sign attached to the red brick exterior. He lets the two-wheeler rest against his leg. He buttons his coat and pulls his Melone down tight.

He looks toward the street, moves his hands to the handlebars, one on each. He places his left foot upon the left pedal. He gives a good push with his right leg, and swings it up and over the seat. He finds the right pedal with his right foot.

And he's off.

He bounces down the curb, keeps his balance on the cobblestones, and begins pedaling. He lifts his head and takes a breath of the fresh evening air. It smells wonderful after all day among vapors of grease and gasoline.

He takes in the late summer sunlight, feeling it on his face. He picks up some speed and leans into a turn—careful with his weight, careful not to slip on the uneven and unpredictable surface.

He loves riding. Pushing his muscles. Cruising through wide streets, over dirt and stone. He slows into another turn. Once through, he finds his cadence again. The speed exhilarates him. It stirs something.

But something else stirs too. It always does on these rides to and from work, twisting and turning through the grid of central Mannheim. He dreams about a vehicle driven not by human muscles or by horses but by an internal combustion engine, not too unlike the ones he builds with Max and Friedrich. A horseless carriage.

The man is Karl Benz, and his dreams are about to kick the whole idea of transportation up a few gears.

● ● ●

Karl Friedrich Michael Vaillant was born in Mühlburg, a small town on the Rhine in southwest Germany. The region is industrial. It's known as "the cradle of the automobile," home to Mercedes-Benz and Porsche, as well as automotive parts behemoths Bosch and Mahle.

But none of those existed the day Karl was born in 1844.

His mother was Josephine Vaillant. His father was Johann George Benz, a railroad engineer. The two married a few months after Karl was born, but Johann died suddenly only two years later. He contracted pneumonia after exhausting himself helping to re-rail an engine that had jumped the tracks. After his death, Josephine changed Karl's surname to Benz, in his honor.

Johann's death impoverished the young family. But Josephine still made sure Karl got an education. He attended local schools, focusing on science and engineering—and did well. At fifteen, he passed the entrance exam for the University of Karlsruhe a few miles away. (The same school, in fact, where Heinrich Hertz would first discover electromagnetic radiation thirty years hence, and inspire a young Guglielmo Marconi.) Karl graduated at nineteen as a mechanical engineer.

But things weren't so simple after that. He tried locksmithing, then working in a factory that built scales, then in one that built locomotives and boilers. He tried working for a company that built bridges. But nothing quite worked out. It's not clear why. Maybe they were just bad fits.

Then in 1870 he met Bertha Ringer, and that fit was good.

Her family was well-to-do. But money didn't matter to her. They fell in love, were engaged, and planned a life together. Karl would move to Mannheim—a close by, but much larger city. Once established, Bertha would join him and they would marry.

In Mannheim, Karl opened the Iron Foundry and Mechanical Workshop with a partner. But that man proved unreliable. The two couldn't get along, and the business began to fail. So Bertha decided to help. She asked her father for both her dowry and her inheritance early. She went to Mannheim, used the money to buy out her fiancé's partner, and she and Karl married. Within a year, their first child was born.

But times remained tough. Having put all Bertha's money toward purchasing the shop, they had little left over with which to begin married life. And when the economy slumped, their shop struggled. They barely kept food on the table. One time, unable to make payments on their growing debt, they had their tools and equipment seized. And in the midst of all this, the couple had two more children.

Karl had to make a change. And he did. He began building engines—the kind that drive industrial machines, undoubtedly like those powering Edison's Invention Factory. And he discovered he was good at it.

A few years later, in 1883, he teamed up with two men who shared his passion for bicycles. They'd owned and run a Mannheim bike shop. The three formed Benz & Cie., with plans to build more engines, and the company began to prosper.

Finally, Karl found his cadence.

Among the forges and anvils, the lathes and planers, the hammers and vices, the heat and smoke of the Benz & Cie. shop, he experimented and built things. He returned to his dream of a horseless carriage. He filed patents for things like the throttle, the ignition, the spark plug, the carburetor, the clutch, the gear shift, and the water radiator. And in 1885 he pulled it all together and introduced the world's first gas-powered automobile—the "Benz Patent-MotorWagen."

His automobile had a frame of steel tubing, three wheels, and wooden cross boards. The wheels had spokes like a bicycle and solid rubber tires. It had one speed, no reverse, and a hand brake. It was difficult to steer (which resulted in some early collisions), but Karl continued to improve it. He added horsepower and better wheels and improved the steering. Finally, on January 29, 1886, he applied for German Patent No. 37435.

Over the next two years, Karl continued working. He loved being in the workshop, caring for his inventions, fixing them, making them better. A true craftsman.

But what he needed to be doing, Bertha knew, was *selling*. The Patent-MotorWagens were ready. Karl just wasn't wired as a salesman. Few people knew about his invention, and those who did were skeptical. Some worried about safety. Indeed, with each road test, he feared being hassled by local police. Others couldn't imagine the usefulness. "If you have a horse," they asked, "why do you need one of these?" Karl harbored doubts too. Were they ready for the public? Did they need more work?

But Bertha had no doubt. Her faith in her husband was unshakable, but she also knew that time was getting by. By 1888 he'd held his patent for two years and sold not a single automobile. Bertha wanted to encourage him, and she wanted to silence critics and skeptics.

So she decided, once again, to help.

BENZ & CIE. AND THE PATENT-MOTORWAGEN
MANNHEIM, GERMANY, 1886

In August of that year, with the children off school, Bertha enlisted Eugen, 15, and Richard, 14, and formulated a plan. They would "borrow" one of Karl's automobiles and drive it sixty-five miles from Mannheim to Pforzheim to visit her mother. It was a huge risk. There were no gas stations along the way—or anywhere else. There were no auto mechanics or tow trucks.

This is how one chronicler described the scene:

> Mother and sons carefully made their way to the factory early in the morning. They quietly pushed the vehicle out of the workshop and only started it once it was a safe distance away from the house—by turning the horizontal flywheel. As the story

goes, she left a note on the kitchen table for [K]arl, who was still asleep, with an openly worded message that she was on her way to Pforzheim—with not a word about the "test drive." He later noticed that the motor car was missing and realized that his loved ones were not travelling by train.[1]

Bertha, a little unsure of the precise route, stopped a lot. Back then gasoline was used as a household cleaner. She could purchase it in pharmacies but only in small quantities. Bertha stopped at three, cleaning out the stock of one. To cool the engine, they stopped for water at public houses, streams, puddles—wherever they could find it. They also had to push the Patent-MotorWagen up and over a few hills. And those same hills caused problems going down. When the brakes wore out, she stopped at a cobbler and had him put leather over the brake shoe—thus inventing brake linings. She cleared a fuel line with a hat pin and insulated an ignition wire with her garter.

And Bertha made it.

The trio reached Pforzheim just after dark. Bertha sent Karl a message by telegraph, letting him know they were safe and the trip had been a success. And after a night's rest, they turned around and drove back home.

Bertha's drive accomplished everything she'd hoped—instant publicity. She'd proved the invention's usefulness and safety. And sales followed. They trickled in at first. But by the end of the decade, they were booming.

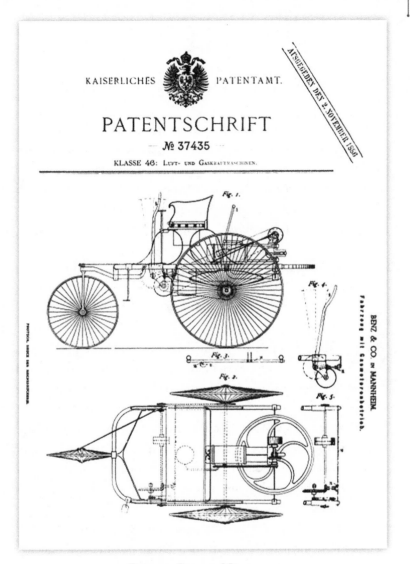

GERMAN PATENT N° 37435:
VEHICLE WITH GAS-ENGINE OPERATION

LiE:

"STOP AND ENJOY LIFE ... LATER."

You've been told: *you have things that need to get done. You have goals. People are counting on you. You haven't got time for things like deep, genuine friendships; sleep and rest; physical exercise; adventure; celebration; worship; prayer; solitude. Not now. Maybe later—but right now, they're distractions. A time sink. Frivolous compared to what you've got going.*

Stay focused. There'll be plenty of time to stop and enjoy life later.

These are lies, and they're holding you back. **Think different.**

• • •

God designs us for work. But that's not all. He also designs us for peace, rest, and restoration. He designs us for activities and experiences *outside* work, for pleasure and joy and rich, restorative things.

These are crucial for physical and mental strength and vitality. Without them we have no chance of becoming the men we're meant to be—robust men leading robust lives holding robust faith.

Crucial though they are, our workaholic culture cautions us against them.

It tells us those kinds of things are for boys and old men—or irresponsible men. It teaches us that during our most "productive years," we should shortchange everything else in favor of whatever will contribute directly to what our culture holds most important: our ascent into achievement and status.

But the consequences of this approach to life are grave. For it's not how we've been designed. And if we ignore ourselves, we can lose ourselves.

We can lose everything.

● ● ●

In the century and a quarter since Benz's invention, the horseless carriage has conquered the world. As the decades rolled on, other engineers and inventors contributed their own modifications and improvements. Those automobiles of old were mere shadows of what the car would become. And while a few thousand rumbling through the mud and dust and cobbles of Europe was a big deal in the late nineteenth century, there are a *million times* that today.

And all those owners know just how quickly their machines can break down. To keep their cars running, owners spend hundreds of billions of dollars every year on maintenance and repair.

We have little choice, right? Cars need it. Rust, corrosion, erosion, deterioration, heat damage, clogs, tears, breaks, ruptures—even the best-made and most durable things break down, eventually. "If you fail to change the oil, no one will fine you or take you to jail," Timothy Keller wrote. "Your car will simply break down because you violated its nature."[2]

How many seasons would a current model year Mercedes-Benz last if its owner neglected all maintenance? Many fewer than the engineers who built it intended, for sure.

Maintenance is imperative.

● ● ●

"God made us: invented us as a man invents an engine."[3]

C. S. Lewis wrote that. But we human beings are more intricate than even the most complex engine—and we need maintenance too. It's *our* nature. It's how our Maker designed us.

So that's exactly what we're going to learn in this chapter. We're going to learn how to obtain maintenance for each of us uniquely.

So much depends upon it—and not just anything will do. God designs us to need *his* maintenance, from *him*.

He makes me lie down in green pastures.
He leads me beside still waters.
He restores my soul. (Ps. 23:2–3)

Imagine an inventor in his workshop—like Benz in Mannheim—apron on, surrounded by tools and spare parts, cleaning his inventions, repairing, oiling, refueling. He's eager and earnest and joyful. Careful. Attentive.

Our Creator God, *our Inventor*, is like that with us. We captivate him. He loves being the One to care for us. Just as he promised the people of Israel in Babylonian exile, "every languishing soul I will replenish" (Jer. 31:25), he will replenish ours too.

If we let him.

● ● ●

The Screwtape Letters by C. S. Lewis, published in 1942, is an imagined peek into the spiritual world, both humorous and frightful. It's a set of correspondences between a senior devil, Screwtape, and a younger, more inexperienced devil, Wormwood. Screwtape offers malevolent advice regarding a "patient," a British man Wormwood is tasked with luring away from God.

In one letter, Screwtape scolds Wormwood for not doing his job very well. He berates him for allowing the patient to do two things, both of which Screwtape considers quite awful:

> On your own showing you first of all allowed the patient to read a book he really enjoyed, because he enjoyed it and not in order to make clever remarks about it to his new friends. In the second place, you allowed him to walk down to the old mill and have tea there—a walk through country he really likes, and taken alone.[4]

Why the strong reaction? Of all the things a fiend could try, keeping a man from reading a book or taking a walk seems so insignificant. There are other things—like tempting him into some great sin—that would seem to have better prospects.

But Screwtape sees it differently.

He tells Wormwood that doing those kinds of things—the book and the walk—allows the patient to feel that he's "coming home, recovering himself." He explains that as a "preliminary to detaching him from the Enemy [that is, God], you wanted to detach him from himself." But because Wormwood allowed the man to read the book and take the walk, says Screwtape, all prior separation-focused work is "undone." All undone! With a book and a walk?

How could two such simple things be so consequential?

> Within Jesus' second commandment, there's actually a third. "You shall love your neighbor as yourself" (Matt. 22:39). Love others. And love them at least as much as you love yourself. Hidden right there in plain sight is permission from our King, Jesus Christ, to love ourselves, to care for ourselves—*or, actually, to allow him to care for us.*

God wires us with desires, interests, motivations, and ambitions. He wires us for certain types of work; but he wires us for certain types of rest, restoration, recreation, and relationship too. He's designed joy, beauty, and connection to be our maintenance.

There are things we're each uniquely built to love. There are activities and experiences we enjoy, not because anyone told us to but because it's how we're designed. And they're as much a part of our true identities as anything else.

They bring *abundance* to our lives. Remember, Jesus promises: "I have come that they may have life, and have it to the full" (John 10:10 NIV). Some fullness comes from the significance and excitement of our work, of course. But much also comes from the things we love.

These things bring sweetness to our lives. They enliven and restore us. They allow us to recover ourselves. They connect us with God too. They bring us close to him in a way that work can't. We get to see him, understand him in new, invigorating ways. By his grace, they deepen our relationship with him. As we spend time in nature, exercise, community, worship, solitude, play, and prayer, we meet him.

He makes us so that we *need* these activities and experiences … and then he blesses us with opportunities to engage in them. *That's* how great God's love is.

And when we engage in them, it gives us confidence. We're able to see in real ways in real time just how much he loves us. We feel it, and we begin to understand.

This whole life—this whole universe—is all about love.

● ● ●

Maintenance is a key part of the pattern God intends for our lives: work, rest, work, restoration, work, recreation, work, relationship. But too many of us ignore it. And like never changing the oil in our automobiles, that feels fine … for a while.

But it isn't fine. Rest and restoration are what maintain our health and balance. We need work, absolutely—but we also need Sabbath.

God modeled the Sabbath pattern when he created the world:

> And on the seventh day God finished his work that he had done, and he rested on the seventh day from all his work that he had done. So God blessed the seventh day and made it holy, because on it God rested from all his work that he had done in creation. (Gen. 2:2–3)

God even made Sabbath a commandment: "Six days you shall labor, and do all your work, but the seventh day is a Sabbath to the LORD your God. On it you shall not do any work" (Ex. 20:9–10). He put it right alongside his commandments to not murder or steal or commit adultery. It's *that* important. But some of us don't believe it. So many of us don't live like it.

Jesus modeled the pattern too, *but he also sharpened our thinking about Sabbath.* He taught us that it's less about specific rules and a specific day of the week and more about the condition and maintenance of our hearts: "The Sabbath was made for man, not man for the Sabbath" (Mark 2:27).

● ● ●

God wants to maintain his people through rest and Sabbath because he loves us. But his love doesn't stop there. He loves *everyone* that much, and he wants to love some people *through us.* But the thing is, he can't do that unless and until we let him love us first. We cannot bless until we've been blessed. We cannot give until we've received.

Just as a Patent-MotorWagen—and every car since—needed periodic cleaning and care, oil, and lubrication to function properly, we need the pattern of rest and Sabbath. Without it we simply can't do the work of our callings very well. And we can't meet our obligations very well either—as husbands, fathers, and friends.

Charles Spurgeon, the "Prince of Preachers," as he was called in nineteenth-century London, said it this way: "It is economy to gather fresh strength.... It is wisdom to take occasional furlough. In the long run, we shall do more by sometimes doing less."[5]

When we engage in maintenance activities and experiences, then our families, our friends, our coworkers, and the world get stronger, more joyful, more powerful, more productive versions of us.

Without maintenance, we can't love as we're meant to love. We can't serve as we're meant to serve. We can't know God or ourselves as we're meant to. But when we're running well and healthy, then we can love and serve other people from a place of abundance, not of depletion, overflowing with the love we've already received.

• • •

Where are you? Does rest and replenishment characterize your life? Or do you sometimes feel like a car running on empty, clogged with dirty oil, with squealing belts and worn tires?

The pace at which most of us live our lives ensures we have little or no time for maintenance. (I used to leave no time for it.) We feel pressure just to keep up. We feel pressure to achieve our goals, to prove ourselves. We're convinced that achievement and status are what are most important. And we schedule every minute such that taking time to come home to God is simply impossible.

So when we think about engaging in activities and experiences outside of work, we ask ourselves—immediately, instinctively—how could we ever find the time? How could we take time from our busy schedules to listen to music or a non-work-related podcast? Or to take a run or a ride in the foothills? Or to go backpacking and fly-fishing? Or to sit on a porch or swing in a hammock? Or to see a movie or drink coffee or beer with non-work friends? How could we be so irresponsible ... so immature?

How responsible is it, though, to disregard a car's maintenance schedule? How mature is it to ignore a car's engine light? It's neither, of course. It's the opposite. It's irresponsible and immature to neglect the important things over which we have ownership and control.

How much more irresponsible and immature is it to neglect ourselves—who are more valuable and wondrous than any machine, and who have more potential?

• • •

What are the consequences of neglecting maintenance? What are the consequences of spurning God's Sabbath pattern and, instead, taking on a pattern that looks like this: work, work, work, work, work, work, work?

We narrow our lives. We eliminate an entire category of things meant to bring us joy and peace and fulfillment. We experience less beauty, less connection. We live less-than-full lives. And everything, even the work we're "prioritizing," suffers.

Henry Ward Beecher, a nineteenth-century abolitionist preacher from Brooklyn, described a world without Sabbath like "a man without a smile, like a summer without flowers, and like a homestead without a garden."[6]

But it gets much worse if we neglect maintenance for too long. Like with a car, neglecting our maintenance will eventually result in breakdown. Anger, anxiety, burnout, depression, despondency, loneliness, isolation, boredom, rebellion, sin—unchecked problems develop into major ones. Ultimately, we can find ourselves in crisis.

Our relationships suffer too, with God and other people. We stop "coming home" to God. We detach. We don't spend time with him. Our relationships with our Inventor—our apprenticeships—become stagnant and stunted.

And because we become depleted, we begin trying to pull what we need from other people. We try to take from them, rather than overflowing love into their lives. If we're married, we try to take from our spouses—things like attention, validation. (I did that.) We talk about "what we need" and "what they're not giving us," rather than letting God love us, fill us, restore us—and then overflowing love onto them.

Bitterness results. Divorce even.

Or maybe we try to take from our kids—validation from grades in school or performances on athletic fields—rather than being filled with God's love, full and restored and overflowing love onto them. Or maybe we try to take from friends, putting ourselves in positions of neediness. We complain they're not doing what we want them to, rather than being full and overflowing love onto them—no matter how they act, no matter what they do for us. (I did those things too.)

Resentment results. Estrangement even.

We break down. Our relationships break down too. And if that's not bad enough, we also blunt our impact on the world beyond family and friends. When we're depleted, we have nothing to give. We go into survival mode. Hoarding and protecting become more important than loving and serving. So, added to the list of things we give up when we neglect maintenance is the significance and excitement, peace and joy that come from engaging in the work of our callings.

Do you ever feel burned out? Sad? Lonely? In survival mode? With nothing to give?

God didn't design us to live like that. He doesn't want us to. Maintenance is a kind imperative. Sabbath is a good commandment. They're blessings—for us ... and for others, *through* us.

● ● ●

Want to feel filled-up? Fully fueled? Overflowing?

The key is moving from the general to the specific, from the theoretical to the practical. Look back at the *Screwtape* examples. Knowing we need rest and refreshment, solitude and beauty—that's general and theoretical. Actually achieving them by reading a book we enjoy and taking a walk alone through an area we like—that's specific and practical.

Or look at Karl Benz. Knowing we need recreation and exercise is general and theoretical. Getting on our bicycles and riding through our home cities or towns? Practical and specific.

And here's another really important thing: these activities and experiences are different for each of us.

So what do they look like for *you*?

Reading in a coffee shop on a rainy day, walking in a park, hiking in the mountains, mountain biking, dirt biking, sleeping under the stars, sleeping in on a Saturday morning, taking a nap on a Sunday afternoon, getting to bed early, getting up early to pray, listening to your favorite worship songs on your commute, working on your car, helping someone else work on theirs, reading Scripture and praying in your car at lunchtime, sitting by a crackling fire, chopping wood, playing golf or softball or pick-up basketball with friends, surfing, walking on a beach, cooking, cooking for others, hosting a dinner, throwing a party, creating art, worshipping God through art, seeing God in art, traveling to foreign countries, writing for a blog and telling your story, writing about God, writing songs or writing poetry, singing in the shower, playing a musical instrument …

You aren't made to imitate; you're made to discover.

If we don't discover these things for ourselves, if we don't let God speak to us and apprentice us into the things that are ours, then we condemn ourselves to the grim task of trying to pull rest, restoration, recreation, relationship—joy, beauty, and connection—from things that can't deliver. Not for us, at least.

But if we do?

If we do, we live more as we're designed to live—in health and balance. We love and serve as we're meant to. We're able to meet our obligations. We're able to do our parts—well and joyfully—in Jesus' grand project of rebuilding this world.

Asking God about these is the fourth fundamental question of identity. And it's our last one before we get to the most important part of the entire book: *getting out there and doing something*.

That'll be the next (and final) chapter.

— SWITCH ON —
"MADE TO REST"
007

God made you to be well—well in mind, body, and spirit. He made you for peace and rest and restoration. He wants you to enjoy your life, to feel his love, to overflow with it.

So run through the questions below, and then let's discover just how you're meant to find *your* maintenance.

Consider these questions and jot down your responses.

007.1   How would you describe your priorities? What's most important to you in your life? Be brutally honest.

007.2   Does how you spend your minutes, hours, and days reflect your priorities? How well?

<< Not So Well -Very Well >>
1   2   3   4   5   6   7   8   9   10

If it could be better, what's being shortchanged?

007.3   Have you ever felt pressure to prioritize work over everything else? Have you ever succumbed? Were there consequences?

007.4   What do you think about the notion that outside-work activities and experiences are among the most important, most responsible, most mature things you can engage in? Describe your reaction.

Discover what maintenance means for you, personally. Complete the activity below. But before you do, take a minute to pray.

Holy Spirit my Counselor, I need your help. I want to go yet deeper into identity. I want to know more. I want to understand how you want to care for me—how you made me to enjoy life and experience Sabbath. But, again, I need your wisdom and knowledge, your ideas and inspiration. I cannot do this without you.

So speak to me. Teach me. As I seek to discover the things that'll bring rest and restoration, recreation and relationship—joy and beauty and connection—help me see what you want me to see. Come Holy Spirit. Come and be my guide. Amen.

Now, pick up a pen or open your tablet or laptop, and write down what you love. Make a maintenance list. Come up with between ten and twenty-five things—things you love doing, things that bring you joy, things that make you feel alive. Don't list anything because it'll cause others to think you're cool or saintly. List things that move your heart, get it beating fast or slow it down. List things that give you rest, restore you, give you recreation, and connect you to God and to other people. Things that allow you to worship him in the doing.

Here's an example. Some of these are on my own maintenance list. Some are not.

- I love seeing and experiencing God's creation, especially mountains, rivers, and streams. I love backpacking. I love standing in a river, fly-fishing.

- I love laughing with family and friends, mostly about simple, silly things.

- I love hanging out with friends. I love a party with good, close friends.

- I love music, especially live music.

- I love a good fire. I love the heat and wonder. I love that we gather around fires, that they encourage friendship and conversation.

- I love cooking and experiencing God's creation through flavors, textures, and smells.

- I love reading and learning new things.

- I love making things. I love crafting things out of wood and metal.

- I love taking long walks, talking with my Father God.

- I love traveling. I love cities. I love the wilderness.

- I love sitting on the beach, bare feet in the sand.

- I love the transparency, boldness, and love of my men's group. I love following Jesus with those men.

- I love being connected to history, through reading and traveling.

- I love praying and listening for the Holy Spirit's voice, especially with my wife.

- I love the smells and tastes of coffee and BBQ. I love how they're both associated with warmth and friendship.

- I love looking up through a leafy tree on a warm, sunny day.

Narrow the list you've created. Look at it, and pray about each item, but do it with eyes open. Listen for God's still small voice. Let the Holy Spirit guide your thoughts as you consider these questions:

007.5   Do the items you wrote down feel right? Accurate?

007.6   Which ones stand out? Which ones strike most true?

007.7   Are there any items that on second look you might want to remove?

Test your list. Does it—along with what you know about the work of your calling—fit within Jesus' two commandments? That is, when you imagine yourself doing the things on your list and pursuing your calling, will God be loved and served first and most? Will you be cared for and filled sufficiently? And will other people be loved and served at least as much as you? Strike any items that get things out of this balance.

Pray one more time.

> *God my Father, Jesus my King, Holy Spirit my Counselor, I want your love and care. I want your rest and Sabbath. But I confess I've sometimes gotten distracted. I confess I've sometimes been too focused on work and forgotten myself. But starting now I choose to think differently about me and about you.*

I want to remember. I want to recover myself. I want to recover my life.

Thank you for how you've made me, how you've designed me for maintenance. Thank you for loving me so much. Thank you for wanting to fill me with your love, to fuel me, to bring me joy and beauty and connection. Thank you for wanting to strengthen me and restore my soul. Thank you for the full life you've promised. I accept that life. I claim it now. Amen.

008

OAK AND STEEL AND ADVENTURE

The man is tall and wiry. He wears his beard long, neatly trimmed. He lifts a stovepipe hat, smooths his hair, and fits it back atop his head. He takes a deep breath. And with his nod, the spectacle begins.

A voice comes up, over the noise of the crowds—the men and women moving through the massive open space, headed toward the exhibits in the wings of the pavilion. It comes from a different man, this one in tails and waistcoat, balding with unruly white curls around the sides.

"Step right up, ladies and gentlemen. Step right up."

It's the voice of a showman. It's clear and carries and calls attention to a hoist—which is now rising, slowly. The contraption is just a crude elevator. An open wooden platform, eight feet by twelve feet, with two vertical guide rails extending fifty feet into the air. But it's bathed in natural light, sitting right under the massive glass and wrought iron dome above.

Only a few people stop—for there's a lot to see in other halls. And this thing, this hoist, is hardly what the fairgoers have come for. This is a worldwide showcase of the newest and greatest industrial achievements—and hoists have been around for millennia.

The man in the stovepipe hat—standing *on* the rising hoist—is unconcerned. He knows he'll have everyone's attention soon enough.

Seconds tick by. A few more people notice and stop and watch. Then a few more. They notice the man rising but also the rope. For the rope, three inches in diameter, is playing an important role.

It connects the hoist to pulleys high above, then comes back down to a drum turning near the ground. As the drum turns, the rope groans and strains and squeaks periodically, as it winds and pulls its load higher. Slowly higher.

The crowd begins to build. The tension does too. With impeccable timing, the showman warns that those prone to fainting might want to have smelling salts at the ready.

At this, a hush falls.

Only then does anyone notice something else. A third man, standing high above, on a platform near the pulleys. And he holds a saber.

The proximity is startling—a saber so close to the toiling rope, the only thing keeping the hoist and its human cargo from crashing to the ground. People nudge one another and point and whisper, until everyone in the massive room is watching the two men aloft.

Just then the platform lurches to a stop. And for the first time, in the silence, the man in the stovepipe hat speaks. From above. Calm and firm.

"Mr. White, please cut the rope."

Muscles freeze. Hearts jump. But the man with the saber doesn't hesitate. He swings over his head and brings the blade around, severing the rope cleanly.

And the hoist plunges.

Muffled screams and gasps.

But then, quite unexpectedly, and in the most ordinary way, it stops—by itself. The hoist's fall is interrupted with a bang and after only a few inches. The man on the platform sweeps his hat off in grand manner and reassures the crowd below.

"All safe, ladies and gentlemen. All safe."

The showman is P. T. Barnum, who'll one day found the world famous Barnum & Bailey Circus. And the event is the Exhibition of the Industry of All Nations—the official name of the 1853–54 New York World's Fair.

But the man above, the man in the stovepipe hat—that's Elisha Otis, and he's going to change skylines the world over.

●　　●　　●

Otis was born in 1811 on a farmstead nestled into the rolling forests of Halifax, Vermont. He was the youngest of six. The farm was prosperous, but he was never a farmer.

He was a tinkerer. Otis preferred metal and machines to soil and seeds. The fields made him restless.

So as soon as he could, he moved sixty miles west to the more urban environment of Troy, New York, right outside Albany. Things were *happening* there, things that interested the young man. In those years, Albany was the tenth largest city in the nation. Networks of new roads and the bustling Hudson River made it a hub of industry and commerce.

Places like Albany needed men like Otis—men adept at building, fixing, and improving things, from carriages to railroad brakes. Men who liked being up to their elbows in axle grease.

For the next few decades, he did a bit of everything. He worked in factories. He helped build and equip them; he helped factories become more efficient. He also started and ran businesses for himself. And interestingly, failures and setbacks never seemed to get him down. Maybe it was his strong Protestant faith.

He built a grist mill. It failed. He converted it to a sawmill. It failed too. But he kept at it. He was a Yankee tinkerer, through and through—even with life. So when someone needed help, he helped. When something needed updating or upgrading, he did it. When a problem needed a solution, he found one. When one business went bankrupt, he started another. And another. And another.

It was in an Albany bed frame factory, where he was master mechanic, that he advanced from tinkerer to inventor. He built an "automatic turner" machine that increased the factory's production fourfold. It enabled an *unskilled* worker to cut fifty bed rails in a day. Prior, a *skilled* craftsman could at most cut twelve.

Despite this, the operation failed. But Otis kept in motion.

When an owner of the ill-fated bedstead business decided to resurrect it in New Jersey, Otis moved there. Then when the owners decided to move it yet again—this time to Yonkers, New York—Otis moved again.

Once there, in Yonkers, Otis saw something that needed improving. (He always did.) The factory had multiple floors—with men, materials, and machines spread between them. Hoists could move things up and down, of course; they were standard equipment at that time. But they were *dangerous*. Ropes and belts could slip or break. And they often did.

So Otis began to ponder and design and build.

What he came up with was an ingenious safety mechanism. To the hoist platform he attached a steel leaf spring, the kind that provided shock absorption to passengers of horse-drawn carriages. To the vertical hoist guides he then fastened ratchet-toothed oak rails.

The principle was simple. A hoisting rope was attached to the center of the spring, and tension from the load on the platform kept the spring flexed and pulled in tight. When pulled in, the spring would not engage the ratchet teeth, and the hoist could travel up and down.

In the event of an accidental fall, though, the leaf spring, having lost tension from the weight of the load, would flatten and jut outward, catching and locking into the ratchet teeth of the guide rails, stopping the fall.

The owner of the Yonkers factory wanted two. For he owned another factory, one in Manhattan, and two workers had recently been involved in a hoist accident there. One man was injured; one

OTIS DEMONSTRATING HIS SAFETY ELEVATOR
CRYSTAL PALACE, NEW YORK CITY, 1854

was killed. And a neighboring Manhattan picture frame factory ordered a third.

Back in Yonkers, though, despite its new location, the bedstead business failed yet again. But once again, ever the indomitable man, Otis took it as an opportunity to try something new. He decided to open his own business on the very same site—this one building his safety hoists, or *elevators*, as they were coming to be called.

Three quick orders notwithstanding, business was slow. The factory made no money for months—not until P. T. Barnum offered Otis one hundred dollars to exhibit his safety elevator at the World's Fair.

He took it, of course. Otis knew he needed to do something bold if his new company was to succeed. But then he decided to do something even bolder. He decided to go to New York City himself, and to promote his product live with his "death drop" stunt.

And it worked. Hundreds of thousands came to the World's Fair during the months it was open. Otis and his compatriots cut the rope every hour, on the hour. And within a year, he'd sold a dozen safety elevators. Within three, he'd sold more than fifty. Within a decade, he'd sold thousands. They were being installed the world over. Eventually the Vatican, the White House, the Empire State Building, Buckingham Palace, the Eiffel Tower, and the Kremlin would all have Otis elevators.

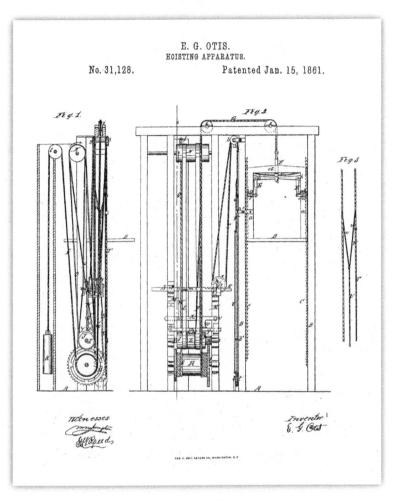

E. G. OTIS.
HOISTING APPARATUS.

No. 31,128.   Patented Jan. 15, 1861.

U.S. Patent Nº 31,128: Hoisting Apparatus

LiE:

"DON'T DO ANYTHING CRAZY."

You've been told: *the world is hard, a dangerous place. Your fears are justified; they're good. They protect you from pain. Let them guide you. Make sure you undertake no endeavor until you're certain of the outcome— because if you do something dumb or impetuous, if you get in over your head, you'll screw up and everyone will know you're a failure for sure.*

Here's the best course: go slow. Play it safe. Don't do anything crazy.

These are lies, and they're holding you back. **Now, *live* different.**

• • •

It all comes to this.

All our prior work leads here: action. *Living it out.*

And all those prior lies—all of them and this one—are meant to prevent it.

Because here's the truth. Becoming the men we're meant to be requires two things: grace and obedience. Grace, the energizing power of God to do what we cannot do on our own. And obedience, our action in alignment with that power.

Loads of grace from God. Action by us. *Living true.*

So that's what we're going to learn in this final chapter, how to take what we've learned and move into action, right now, the right way.

God's ready with as much grace as we'll ever need, but we must be ready to act. For no matter how much we *know* of our true identities—and at this point we know a lot—we'll never *become* those identities if we don't live into them. Into confidence. Into significance. Into passion. Into relationship. Into life as we were truly made to live it.

But once again culture is set against us. In hundreds of ways, the voices around us encourage conformity. Timidity. Our culture fosters fear of failure. Of hardship. Of embarrassment. Of not fitting in.

Think of your own biggest fears. What keeps you awake at night? Culture reminds us about things like job security, financial security, retirement security. *Worry*, it urges. *Be afraid. Play it safe. Don't be irresponsible.* And we listen. (I sure have.)

But we don't have to. We're descended from renegades and revolutionaries, change-makers, and troublemakers—men and women who imagined and risked and challenged, who explored and created and changed the world.

It's not that our forebears didn't fear. They surely did, feeling all the same things we do. But the ones who were able to change the world didn't let fear stop them. They kept their fears in perspective and proper order.

Okay, what does that mean for us? Perspective? Proper order?

Well, it means we're designed to fear. It means fear is okay. But it also means we're designed to fear *some things* much more than others. And what we should fear most as followers of Jesus is God himself.

We should fear living apart from him and outside of his intentions.

That should keep us awake.

We should fear living less than the fullness our Maker intends for us. We should fear missing out on what life's *really* about. We should fear spending our lives for things that don't actually matter.

Those kinds of things should haunt us.

For what matters most, to any of us, is what God's doing—in the world and in our lives. Once he's revealed some of that to us—who we're meant to be, how his gracious power is meant to flow through us, how we're meant to live as part of his plan—our greatest fear should be missing even a minute of that astounding opportunity.

Is there risk? Absolutely. Could there be pain and hardship? Yes. Will something amazing happen? Undoubtedly.

"Here is the world," wrote Frederick Buechner. "Beautiful and terrible things will happen. Don't be afraid."[1]

He's right. And don't.

We don't need to be afraid of what might happen to us in this world because God is with us … always. He's the most powerful force in the universe—by such an extent that we can't even fathom it—and he's on our side. He's working right alongside us and right *inside* us.

And though there may be pain ahead, he's secured the ultimate outcome. Jesus Christ, our King, his Son, did that. So we know how the story of history ends. We know how *our* stories end. With new beginnings for us and the world, restoring our Inventor's original, perfect design for all things.

As loyal apprentices, we can trust the watchful supervision of our Master. We can trust that any failure or hardship, any embarrassment or alienation will serve only to build our character. (I'm beginning to do that.)

We can trust that failure—even if we're as practiced at it as Elisha Otis was—can make us smarter. Stronger. More patient. We can trust that humiliation will make us more humble, more powerful. We can trust that hardship will make us more grateful, more merciful. We can trust that alienation will allow us to learn to turn to Father God who'll never leave, never fail, never let us down.

So we must move beyond, above timidity. We must live forward, fearless toward the things of the world, ready when our Designer calls. We must move beyond, above conformity—confident and ready to step into new things.

We must trust this: that the biggest risk, actually, is doing nothing.

"Let us get to acts and deeds," preached Charles Spurgeon.[2]

Yes, let's. It's time.

"Make a careful exploration of who you are and the work you have been given," the apostle Paul implored the Galatians, "and then sink yourself into that" (Gal. 6:4 THE MESSAGE).

Integrity is everything. We can count on machines with integrity. Passengers riding the seventy-three Otis elevators that hang in the Empire State Building can count on them, whooshing up and down, because they have integrity. Everything is aligned—their purpose, design, manufacture, use.

But if anything gets out of alignment—or is never put into alignment in the first place—integrity vanishes. An invention might be well-designed and well-built, for example, but it'll still lack integrity unless and until it's actually put to the *use* for which it's intended. An Otis elevator would have no integrity if someone tried to use it as, say, a boat.

The same is true of us. And now is the time to pull everything in our lives completely into alignment. It's time to begin living with integrity. To live in harmony with our design.

What does that look like?

Well, take a look back at the work we've done already—we pondered our designs, our talents, our gifts, our names, our functions, our callings, the ways we're meant to be maintained, and cared for. All these things—all of them—are in alignment already. God does that.

And they await *us* … *you.* They await us *living true.* For unlike an elevator, God allows us to choose our uses. He allows us to choose our actions. Living with integrity, in alignment with our Inventor's will, is not a given. *We must choose it.*

Thomas Merton, Trappist mystic and monk, put it like this: "God leaves us free to be whatever we like. We can be ourselves or not, as we please. We are at liberty to be real, or to be unreal. We may be true or false, the choice is ours."[3]

God allows us to choose how we spend our days. He lets us choose to step into true identity. He lets us choose to live according to our deepest truths.

Or … not.

But what will you choose?

• • •

Why was Otis's death drop so unforgettable for fairgoers? Because they got to see the full potential of his invention in action. They got to see an amalgamation of parts transform, become something greater, become something that in its own humble way could change the world.

In one slashing moment, they got to see what those bits and pieces of wood and metal and hemp were meant for. They saw its lifesaving purpose revealed in a short drop and a sudden stop.

A collection of disconnected parts is dead, divided. But when brought into alignment, those parts become a whole and come to life with new purpose and significance. And it's a very big deal—first action. It's a very big moment. An invention, when it begins to be what it's meant to be, it goes in a sense from death to life. It enters into a new kind of existence.

It's the moment Edison's filament gleamed for the first time, the moment Marconi's signal first came hurtling over the horizon, the moment the Wright's plane first pushed into the wind over Kill Devil Hills, the moment Daguerre's image first came into view, the moment Bell's voice first crackled through the telephone receiver, the moment Bertha Benz and her sons took off through the back roads of Germany.

It was the moment Elisha Otis's device first caught a *real* falling elevator and in a single breathless moment *actually* saved a person's life.

That could be your moment.

But are you ready?

• • •

The best way to create such moments is to ask simply, "What's the bold move?"

This forces us to devise actions, deeds in alignment with true identity, acts that demonstrate our trust in God—in whatever situations we find ourselves now.

Bold moves bring us to life. Full life. They get us *living true*.

Elisha Otis was a master of the bold move. His life was full of actions taken in the face of uncertainty and despite fear, whether it was moving geographically, starting a new business, or moving into a new industry. But his boldest move, of course, was to demonstrate his safety elevator in singular manner. And with it, with his daring death drop stunt, he launched a multibillion dollar company and a new way of building cities.

Bold moves allow us to *become* our true identities. When we make them, we counter doubts. We face fears. We negate our negativity. *We simply become ourselves.*

Such moves bring us into full alignment. They give us integrity.

But how do we find them? The right ones?

Usually they've found us already. For the best bold moves are often right there, *right here*, right in front of us.

So all we have to do to begin *really living, living true*, is to ask in whatever circumstances we find ourselves what would men do here, men with identities like ours? What *should* men do here, men with spiritual gifts like ours, with names like ours, with callings like ours?

And then we can simply begin doing those things one by one.

We can stare fear long in the face and embrace our heritage—we can, ourselves, become rebels and revolutionaries, change-makers and troublemakers.

> The LORD is on my side; I will not fear.
> What can man do to me? (Ps. 118:6)

We can start small. We can start with one person. We can simply ... *begin.*

Now, are you ready?

— SWITCH ON —
"MADE TO LIVE"
008

God's ready for you to live true. He's desperate for you to focus your life. To live with intentionality and momentum. Purpose and power. To be confident and brave.

If you're ready too, jump right into the questions below. Then let's figure out your next move—*and we'll make it a bold one.*

Sketch your personal blueprint. This will be your key takeaway from this chapter and this book. Your personal blueprint will be the framework through which you can run life's decisions. It'll serve as your life map, your written guide going forward.

But first, take a moment to pray.

> *God my Father, Jesus my King, Holy Spirit my Counselor, thank you for how you've made me. Thank you for everything you've given me, for how you've prepared me. Thank you for how you've blessed me with talents and gifts, with a true name, with a place and a position in your work of loving and serving, and in your grand project of restoring the world.*
>
> *Thank you for filling me with your love, for fueling me, for strengthening me and restoring my soul. Thank you for loving me so much.*
>
> *I want to turn your love—and my love—into action. I'm ready. I want to begin living true. But I need your*

help. Speak to me now. Help me see what you see. Amen.

Okay, now let's get to it. Let's pull everything together.

Use the worksheet in the pages following. It'll help you condense things. Arrange them a bit. But most importantly, it'll allow you to see everything in one place. And what will emerge as you fill it out is the most complete picture possible—right now—of your true identity.

YOUR PERSONAL
BLUEPRINT

What natural talents did you identify in chapter 4?

- _____
  _____

- _____
  _____

- _____
  _____

- _____
  _____

- _____
  _____

What spiritual gift(s) did you identify in appendix A? Put a star next to any primary gifts. Draw an arrow from any secondary gifts, pointing to the gifts they might be meant to support.

- _____
  _____

- _____
  _____

- _____
  _____

Do you think any of your spiritual gifts are meant to be stacked upon any of your natural talents? Which ones? How might they work together?

_____
_____
_____
_____
_____
_____
_____

Did you hear a true name in chapter 5? What was it? If not, did you adopt one of the true names suggested, one of the ones pulled directly from Scripture? Which one?

_____
_____

What were the key points from the *calling funnel* exercise in appendix B, especially from the "our hearts," the "our remade hearts," and the "our experiences" sections? Sketch them below.

_____
_____
_____
_____
_____

_____

_____

Using the *calling funnel* in appendix B, did you get an idea for what your unique calling might be? Describe it here.

_____

_____

_____

_____

_____

_____

_____

List the items from your *maintenance list* from chapter 7. Write them below.

- _____
- _____
- _____
- _____
- _____
- _____
- _____
- _____
- _____
- _____
- _____
- _____
- _____
- _____
- _____

- _____
- _____
- _____

Pray but with eyes open and pen in hand. Sit back. Look at your completed blueprint. Listen for God's still small voice. Let the Holy Spirit guide your thoughts as you consider these questions and jot down your answers:

008.1   What themes emerge? What patterns? What are the common threads among your gifts, your name, your story, your calling? Write down whatever you see.

008.2   What comes to mind when you think about what lies ahead for you, in true identity? What do you think God might have for you over the next ten to twenty years of your life given your gifts, your name, your story, your calling? Spend a few minutes thinking, dreaming a bit, writing a bit.

008.3   What comes to mind when you think about how you might begin living in true identity—*right now, right where you are, right in your current circumstances*? What thoughts surface when you think about what's most important at this moment, most pressing?

- Is it to begin developing a particular spiritual gift?
- Is it to seek healing—through a round of counseling, perhaps—from something in your past that you've ignored too long?
- Is it a confession to a friend about something that's been too long hidden?

- Is it training in the skills required for the work of your calling?

- Is it simply to begin that work?

- Is it to begin engaging on a more regular basis in some or all of your rest and Sabbath items?

Formulate a bold move. Okay, we're finally here. Based upon your answers above, brainstorm about a potential action. Pick one. Pick something you can do right now, this week. Pick something you can measure. Tell a friend about it and ask him or her to keep you accountable. Then go do it. Go for it!

And after you do, formulate another and do it too. And then another. And another.

Pray one more time.

> *God my Father, Jesus my King, Holy Spirit my Counselor, I resolve to stay faithful to my apprentice-ship. I declare that I want to become the man you intend me to be. I will neither forget nor neglect what I've discovered about myself so far, and I will continue listening for your voice and looking for your guidance.*
>
> *I resolve to live differently. I resolve to develop my gifts. I resolve to "put on" my true name, more and more—in more areas of my life, in more circumstances. I resolve to begin the work of my calling. I resolve to continue making bold moves, to complete those you've put on my heart already and to complete those you will put on my heart in the future. And I resolve to press on, even when it's hard and frustrating.*
>
> *I love you that much. Amen.*

SPIRITUAL GIFTS

The apostle Paul wrote more about spiritual gifts than any other biblical author. His lists of possible gifts appear in three chapters: Romans 12; 1 Corinthians 12; and Ephesians 4. None of his lists is exhaustive. Each is different but overlapping with the others. Along with a few other scriptural passages, his lists give a framework for thinking about our gifts.

Paul's lists are combined into a single list below with descriptions added.

As you read the list, keep these points in mind:

- All work energized by the Holy Spirit is accomplished by and through a spiritual gift, whether that gift is listed here or not. This list is therefore meant to offer examples of the *kinds of things* that can be gifts of the Holy Spirit.

- The descriptions below are intended to help you see your gifts, but they may not be precise. There's nothing rigid about how gifts emerge in our lives, except in outcome (they always pass the love of God forward).

None of us need to fit anyone else's picture of what it looks like to embody a particular gift. You need not become someone else. You must become more you.

- The descriptions are idealized. Only Jesus embodied the gifts fully. No one else will reflect all the attributes or abilities listed, nor will anyone else reflect any of them perfectly. For the rest of us, the descriptions are aspirational, meant to call us to rise up into our truer selves.

- Because Jesus embodies each one fully and perfectly, the gifts below are separated into three categories— priest, prophet, king—the three general functions Jesus performs for us. Since he calls us into his work, it's useful for us to think in these terms as we examine our own gifting.

- It's possible for you to have multiple gifts. You might have primary and secondary gifts, that is, the degree to which you have one gift may be greater than the degree to which you have another. And if you do have multiple gifts, they'll likely overlap one another, work together, support one another, modify one another.

- If you struggle to identify your gifts, don't worry. Just begin experimenting with different kinds of service. Look for opportunities to try the various kinds of work described below. Have fun. Take some risks. And as you do, be on the lookout for the Holy Spirit's energizing power.

Read the list and the descriptions. Before you do, grab a notebook and a pen, or be ready to take notes on your computer, tablet, or phone. And as you encounter each gift, ask yourself three questions:

- Is it familiar? Does it describe you? Does it describe how, at some point, you've worked to love and serve and impact other people?

- Did you feel the presence and power of the Holy Spirit in you, in the work?

- Did you feel significance, excitement, peace, and/or joy from the work?

If it becomes clear that a particular gift doesn't apply to you—go ahead and skip to the next one. But when the answers to the three questions above come together in the work of a particular spiritual gift, write down the name. When you're done, you should have a short list of possible gifts. **With it, you'll be able to complete the activities at the end of this appendix.**

● ● ●

PRIESTLY GIFTS: FOR MEETING THE NEEDS OF OTHERS

Exhortation
(Romans 12:3–8)

Exhortation is sometimes called "encouragement" or "counseling." It is those, but it goes beyond them too. The word *exhortation* in Romans 12:8 comes from the Greek verb *parakaleó*, which can mean "to call to one's side," "to speak to," "to entreat or beseech," "to admonish," "to comfort or console," "to encourage or strengthen or motivate," or "to instruct or teach." So the gift of exhortation is the ability to have personal conversations—tough ones, when needed, but edifying and inspiring ones too.

People with this gift care fiercely. They're willing to pursue people in need and intervene in their lives. But they do so appropriately. They're assertive, not aggressive.

Some examples of people needing exhortation are those struggling with depression, facing severe loss, unable to overcome fear, caught by an addiction, wavering in their faith, or who have strayed completely. So all of us need it at one time or another—and many of us will need it multiple times.

Giving
(Romans 12:3–8)

The gift of giving is the Spirit-empowered ability to share resources, time, and physical energy to meet the practical needs of other people. We're all called to give, but people with this gift do it exceptionally. The Greek adverb used to describe how these people give is *haplós*, which means "simply," "sincerely," "graciously," or "bountifully." These people might build houses or churches or schools or dig wells. They might provide food to people who need food or distribute clothing to people who need clothing. Or they might donate money to people and organizations doing God's work.

People with this gift are not necessarily rich in material resources. (Jesus didn't choose a rich person when he wanted to give us an example for how to give, see Mark 12:41–45). But they see themselves as stewards of God's resources, and they have supernaturally generous hearts. They give sacrificially, expecting nothing in return. Being part of God's work is their reward.

Helps
(1 Corinthians 12:27–31)

The gift of helps is the ability to assist other people in the work of *their* spiritual gifts. The Holy Spirit gives these people a supercharged ability to support other people, to work behind or alongside others in *their* work for God.

People with this gift relieve the burdens of others, freeing them to move more powerfully in their giftings, in their callings. They're joyful support. And they tend to have a good sense of how, when, and where to help. They know what'll be truly helpful, and what'll just be counterproductive.

They are comfortable to work wherever needed, and they're pleased to submit to the vision and direction of others. They're easy to trust. They're loyal. They're dependable. They say *yes* quickly. They jump in and take ownership, but they don't usurp the work given by God to someone else. They tend not to criticize. They're comfortable doing hard work unseen. And so, by the power of the Holy Spirit, they magnify the efforts of countless people.

Hospitality
(1 Peter 4:8–10; Romans 12:9–13)
This is the Spirit-given ability to welcome others—friends, strangers, anyone—offering friendship, warmth, comfort, connection, and food. We're all called to be hospitable, but people with this gift are energized with a special openness and kindness. They host joyfully and sacrificially.

People with this gift aren't judgmental, confrontational, or pushy. They push no agenda, other than one of welcome. They simply want to provide a place of rest and relaxation and restoration, open to anyone—a safe haven, a place of peace.

They tend to make friends easily. They put people at ease. They're good at networking, connecting people. They are, in fact, what holds together many extended relationships.

Intercession
(James 5:13–18; 1 Timothy 2:1–2)
This gift is the ability to petition God on behalf of others, consistently and earnestly. We're all supposed to pray for one

another. "Jesus Christ carries on intercession for us in heaven; the Holy Ghost carries on intercession in us on earth; and we the saints have to carry on intercession for all men," wrote Oswald Chambers, that old Scottish soul (and perhaps best-ever writer of devotions).[1] But the Holy Spirit energizes people with the gift of intercession with a special ability for this kind of prayer.

People with this gift enter God's presence and ask him to help, and they want to do it on behalf of others. For they understand the urgency and immediacy of the spiritual battle raging around us, and so they're compelled to pray, to intercede. And because they pray with true hearts and consistently and determinedly pray for God's will, they see frequent and specific answers to their prayers—though not always the answers they or we expect.

Mercy
(Romans 12:3–8)
The Greek words for the gift of mercy are *eleon en ilarotati*, which translate as "mercy in hilarity." *Ilarotati* is the Greek root of the English word *hilarity*. The words also translate as "mercy in cheerfulness." So the gift of mercy is the ability to bring compassion and help to people who need it and to do it with gladness and joy. We're all called to be merciful, of course, but these people are energized for it in a special way by the Holy Spirit. And they can bring help and compassion consistently over the long term.

People with this gift are physical manifestations of God's merciful love. They're drawn like magnets to people in need. They don't focus only on people easy to serve, but on people who are truly hurting. They love and serve people others tend to forget. They're not judgmental. They harbor no sense of superiority. They identify with the people they serve. They understand we're all needy; we're all sinners, guilty and wretched; we're all in need of mercy and love.

Pastoring
(Ephesians 4:11–14)

The Greek word for this gift is *poimén*, which translates as "shepherd." Shepherds spend time with their sheep. They protect and care for them as they grow, tend to them when sick or wounded, find them when lost. So the gift of pastoring is the ability to do this for people—to take responsibility for them, to guide them into maturity as they grow into the character of Jesus.

People with this gift spend time and energy on people already following Jesus, so they pick up where evangelists leave off. They have good sense for next steps, for what people need now, in order to grow, whether it's prayer, discipleship, study, solitude, confession and repentance, accountability, service, or something else. They walk alongside people, but they also walk ahead and live by example. They lead and influence, but not from a distance. They connect one-on-one. They stick with people through ups and downs, through times of crisis and times of blessing and in between.

Service
(Romans 12:3–8)

The gift of service is simply the supercharged ability to work for the good of others. The Greek word used in Romans 12 is *diakonia*, which translates as "waiting tables." In a broader sense, it translates as "service," "ministry," or "ministration." People with this gift serve "by the strength that God supplies" (1 Pet. 4:10–11). They do for others what they cannot do for themselves; they do for others what no one else wants to do for them.

People with this gift work hard and quietly, without fanfare. They're willing to do whatever is needed, humbly—think waiting tables. They work with kindness and love and without resentment. They respect and honor people with their work—all people. And they're able to serve over long periods of time because they serve out of purpose rather than obligation.

This gift overlaps with the gift of helps, but it's less focused on supporting a particular *person* in his or her gifts and more focused on furthering a particular mission or cause or project. It also overlaps with the gift of mercy but is perhaps less specifically focused on easing human suffering. And it's often combined with other gifts— maybe all gifts—but especially the service-oriented gifts.

● ● ●

PROPHETIC GIFTS: FOR SPEAKING TRUTH

Discernment
(1 Corinthians 12:4–11)

Some things are from God; some aren't. Some things are true; some aren't. And not everything is what it seems. Discernment is the gift to be able to determine whether certain things people do, say, or believe are rooted in the truth and work of God, or whether they're rooted only in the things of man or the work of the Enemy. The word for this gift in 1 Corinthians 12 is *diakrisis*, which translates as "distinguishing"— between good and evil, light and darkness. People with this gift are energized by the Holy Spirit to stand guard. They watch and protect.

The gift of discernment is not just about accumulating knowledge of Scripture. The gift rests upon that foundation, but discernment is more than just knowledge. It's a divine empowerment to understand and internalize the truth and teaching of Jesus—and then to see what others do not. It's also a divine empowerment to sense the presence and promptings of the Holy Spirit in the moment—and to sense the presence of evil. (That's not to say, though, that these people are infallible. They've just proven trustworthy, over time.)

Evangelism
(Ephesians 4:11–14)

The gift of evangelism is the ability to tell non-Christians about Jesus in a way that helps them become his followers. The Greek word for those with this gift is *euaggelistes*, which translates as "one who brings good news"—the best news any of us will ever hear. The hearts of people with this gift break for those who are lost, and they want to tell them about Jesus.

Because their hearts are for non-Christians, people with this gift tend to spend much of their time and energy away from the church, out in the secular world. They're often at work in places where people are most lost and most desperate for God—homeless shelters and addiction recovery programs, conference rooms and corner offices. They're comfortable in places like that, more comfortable, perhaps, than in their local church.

Knowledge
(1 Corinthians 12:4–11)

The gift of knowledge is the ability to discover, compile, analyze, clarify, bring insight to, and otherwise make good use of information and ideas in the Bible, of course, but in other areas too. People with this gift are energized by the Holy Spirit to study and research and learn. Through them, we gain deeper understanding of God, ourselves, and our world.

The two Greek nouns used for this gift are *logos* and *gnósis*. The second simply translates as "knowledge." The first, though, can be translated as "divine utterance," confirming that the gift isn't about accumulating knowledge for knowledge's sake or for our own sake. Rather, it's about being led by God into knowledge *for the sake of others*. And people with this gift perform that function with humility.

They are curious and observant and tend to learn easily. They like to read, experience things, investigate, go deep. They look at data, issues, and ideas from different perspectives. They're unafraid of truth, and nothing's off-limits. They're careful too in their research, in keeping things within the principles of Scripture, and in present-ing knowledge to others. They know that misunderstandings, misin-terpretations, mental confusions, and mistaken beliefs can have dire consequences.

Prophecy
(1 Corinthians 12:4–11; Ephesians 4:11–14; Romans 12:3–8)

The gift of prophecy is the ability to hear God's voice and to commu-nicate it to others. People with this gift are empowered by the Holy Spirit to reveal his truth in real time—whenever and wherever it's needed. Their role, explained A. W. Tozer, is to "see with an anointed eye and to tell out what God has to say for a given time."[2]

The gift of prophecy is not the *office of prophet*. Prophets of the Old Testament, the biblical authors, held the office. Because the Canon of Scripture is now closed, though, the office exists no longer. But the spiritual gift of prophecy remains, though its function is nar-rower. The role of people with this gift is to hear from God in a way that fills out Scripture but fits within it too. They're supercharged to hear his voice but not in a way that contradicts or supersedes biblical truth. And, of course, these people are fallible. Their words, like any-one else's, must be tested.

Teaching
(1 Corinthians 12:27–31; Ephesians 4:11–14; Romans 12:3–8)

The gift of teaching is the ability to help people learn things that increase and strengthen faith. The Greek noun in 1 Corinthians 12 is *didaskalos*, which means "teacher" or "master." People with this gift are energized by the Holy Spirit to explain things in a way that people understand.

People with this gift are good communicators. They tend to be articulate and engaging. They're curious and observant too. They enjoy gaining knowledge. And because there's no subject beyond the reach of God, the subject matter of their teaching can be anything. But it's always and ultimately founded on the truth of Jesus.

They may teach on a small scale, one-on-one or in small groups, or on a larger scale. They may teach any age group—in a classroom, from a pulpit, or behind a podium at conferences or retreats. They may do it by writing books, writing blogs, or creating video or audio. However they do it, they're successful. People learn from them.

Tongues/Interpretation of Tongues
(1 Corinthians 12:4–11)

The gift of tongues is the supernatural ability to speak in a language one hasn't learned. This can happen, possibly, in two ways—but there's a ton of mystery here and many differing opinions. The unknown language can be, perhaps, a foreign one—one the speaker hasn't learned (as in Acts 2:5–11). Or apparently, it can be a language of heaven or of the angels (as in 1 Cor. 13:1; 14:2).

The gift of interpretation of tongues is the ability to understand and make known what's spoken in tongues, even though the language spoken is also not known to the interpreter (as in 1 Cor. 14).

The purposes of these gifts, like all gifts, are love and service. If the gift of tongues is used to speak a known human language, known to the hearers but not to the speaker, the purpose is evangelism, to reach people with the message of Jesus despite language barriers. If the gift of tongues is used to speak a heavenly language, the purpose is to convey the heart of God, to build up others, strengthening faith.

When a person with the gift of tongues speaks a heavenly language in a gathering, someone with the gift of interpretation must be present so the hearers can understand what's being said. There's no question that the combination of tongues and interpretation can be employed "for the benefit of all" (1 Cor. 14:5 THE MESSAGE). It's simply another method by which human beings can offer knowledge, teaching, and/or prophecy to one another.

But because the work associated with these gifts is mysterious and unfamiliar, it can also be an obstacle for some and therefore must be engaged carefully. When it is, Paul cautioned, it should only be engaged in small groups of two or three people and, again, "only if someone is present who can interpret" (1 Cor. 14:27 THE MESSAGE).

People with these gifts don't use them for self-satisfaction or self-glorification. And they know they are fallible. Their words must also be tested.

● ● ●

KINGLY GIFTS: FOR LEADING OTHERS

Administration
(1 Corinthians 12:27–31)

The gift of administration is the ability to bring order out of chaos. The Greek word used in 1 Corinthians 12 is *kubernésis*, meaning "steering" or "piloting." These people can execute strategy and accomplish goals. They care about details, precision, promptness, doing things properly and in an orderly manner. They're empowered by the Holy Spirit to *get it done*, whether the task is big or small.

This gift may include any or all of the following skills or abilities: strategic planning, tactical adjusting, goal setting, problem solving, team building, organizational skill, operational skill, the ability to manage a budget or keep a schedule, and the ability to find and deploy resources.

People with this gift sacrifice themselves for others by providing help and leadership. Without them projects and organizations would run less efficiently and less work would be done.

The Gift of the Apostle
(1 Corinthians 12:27–31; Ephesians 4:11–14)

The gift of the apostle is the ability to explore new territory, to find a new approach, to create and build something new. People with this gift are energized by the Holy Spirit to be God's pioneers and entrepreneurs. The word *apostle* comes from the Greek word *apóstolos*, which means "one who is sent."

People with this gift are adaptable. They love learning and experiencing new things. They tend to be good leaders. They're able to inspire and rally people to execute a mission. They're able to draw out gifts in other people. But they tend to be better starters than long-term leaders—unless they also possess the gift of leadership. If they do not, they'll often at some point pass a maturing mission or organization off to a gifted leader. Doing that frees them to move on and begin again.

It's important to note that, like with prophecy, the spiritual gift of the apostle is not the same as the *office of apostle*. The apostles of the New Testament, biblical authors, held the office. As the Canon is closed, the office no longer exists. But the gift remains.

Faith
(1 Corinthians 12:4–11)

The gift of faith is the ability to trust that God will do what he says he'll do—and to help other people to trust that too. People with this gift have a unique confidence in God's promises, in his goodness and power. Trust is in their bones. Their thinking, therefore, tends to be clear, less susceptible to the influence of lies and unhealthy doubt.

People with this gift believe that when God says he'll take care of us, he will. They believe that when God tells us he has good plans for us, he does. They believe that when God tells us nothing can separate us from his love, nothing can. They believe that when God says we're forgiven and loved, we actually are. They trust his will and believe it'll be accomplished, even when it seems impossible.

They tend to be calm in demeanor and convincing in words. They're people on whom we can rely in tough times, lean times, and times of crisis. They bolster our faith and keep us from believing lies of the Enemy. They get us to dream. They get us to act and take risks.

Healing
(1 Corinthians 12:4–11)

The gift of healing is the ability to be an intermediary for God, through whom he works to heal people who are sick and suffering, physically. The Greek words denoting this gift in 1 Corinthians 12 are *charismata iama*. *Iama* translates as "healing." *Charisma* translates as "a gift of grace, an undeserved favor."

People with this gift have strong faith, believing that God is supremely powerful and can heal whomever he wants, whenever he wants. And they have a special compassion for the sick, for people with physical ailments or handicaps, for those who are hurting or dying.

They get excited about seeing physical healing—but not to get credit themselves. They just want people restored, and they want God to get credit. They get excited about talking to others about the things they've seen, how they've seen God's power.

And they can verify people have been healed through their prayers—though they don't see people healed every time they pray. They might not even see it very often. "They are miracles, not ordinaries," wrote Philip Yancey.[3] But their gift is real, a special sign of God's restoring power.

Leadership
(Romans 12:3–8)

Leadership is the gift to be able to lead others toward the accomplishment of God's will. The Greek verb used in Romans 8 is *proistemi*, which translates as "to preside" or "to rule over" or "to direct." People with this gift can form and communicate a vision, unite and motivate people, and keep them working harmoniously toward the accomplishment of that vision.

People with this gift are comfortable being out front. They tend to gravitate there, in fact. They're comfortable making decisions and taking responsibility. They inspire the rest of us to dream and learn and become better. They're good at getting us to rise up, to do our best. Gifted leaders also have staying power. They're able to make long-term commitments and remain in positions of leadership for substantial periods of time.

They love and serve others by leading them. They sacrifice by taking on the responsibility of leading, and they do it according to scriptural principles. They don't do it to get validation, nor do they abuse their positions. They also know they're fallible, so they're humble too. And the rest of us are confident in their leadership. We trust them and follow.

Miracles
(1 Corinthians 12:4–11)

The gift of miracles is the ability to be an intermediary through whom God works supernaturally to perform special acts that reveal his presence, goodness, and power. The Greek words denoting this gift are *energéma* and *dynameon*. *Energéma* translates as "a working." *Dynameon* translates as "deeds showing power" or "marvelous works." Ultimately, like with the gift of healing, God's purpose with this gift is to bolster the faith of his followers and to help people who aren't yet his followers become them.

People with this gift have a special interest in helping others see God through miraculous events—which, according to Dallas Willard, are "extraordinary events or powerful effects not easily attributable, if attributable at all, to merely natural causes."[4] Miracles happen, wrote Willard, when what "you would expect to happen in the course of nature does not happen because God has intervened."[5]

While they know miracles aren't common, these people trust that God sometimes does them, so they simply ask him to do more. And while they can verify—on some level—that miracles have happened through their prayers, people with this gift know they're not in control of when, where, or how God performs them.

Wisdom
(1 Corinthians 12:4–11)

The gift of wisdom is the ability to bring insight and guidance to other people—individuals, groups, organizations—and into specific situations in order to help them make good decisions. The words denoting this gift are the Greek nouns *logos* and *sophia*. The first translates as "divine utterance." The second as "wisdom." People with the gift of wisdom have good sense and sound judgment, both empowered by the Holy Spirit.

People with this gift help the rest of us cut through complexity, confusion, and conflict. They help us see the way forward. They're able to apply biblical truth to tough problems and complicated questions—maybe financial or relational, maybe parenting decisions, professional decisions, or organizational decisions. It can be anything in the world.

These people typically have strong command of Scripture. But the gift of wisdom is more about being able to *apply* that truth, than it is about possessing it in the abstract. Knowing biblical truth is the gift of knowledge. Knowing how to apply that truth to a person's life—that's the gift of wisdom.

— SWITCH ON —

Compare your list of spiritual gifts to the list of natural talents you made at the end of chapter 4. Pray about both with eyes open and pen in hand. Listen for God's voice. Look at your lists, your notes and notations, as you pray. Let the Holy Spirit guide your thoughts as you consider these questions:

A.1   Do the gifts and talents listed feel right, accurate?

A.2   What stands out? What strikes most true?

A.3   Are there any that, on second look, you might need to reconsider?

A.4   Did you generate any ideas about *other* possible gifts you might possess not listed here? If so, write out your own descriptions.

A.5   Could any of your spiritual gifts be stacked on top of any of your natural talents? Which ones? How might they work together?

Pray one more time.

> *God my Father, Jesus my King, Holy Spirit my Counselor, thank you for how you've made me—a custom-designed, one-of-a-kind masterpiece. Thank you for the care you took in my design. Thank you*

for revealing some of that design today. Thank you for showing me who I am, truly.

I confess I've doubted myself, wondering if I was good enough. I confess I've doubted how you designed me. I confess I've doubted you. But now I bring those doubts to you. And I repent them. I choose to turn my back on those old, sour beliefs. I choose to believe them no more. I choose to think differently.

I choose to believe you, and I declare confidence in myself and my design—how I am, how you made me, and who you mean me to become. Amen.

CALLING FUNNEL

From Scripture we know our callings, generally. We know we're all called to this: loving and serving others by the power of the Holy Spirit for God's epic and eternal purpose of reinventing this world.

But what about our callings *specifically* and *personally*?

Fortunately, God speaks about this too, not just through Scripture but also straight into our very lives. Our *gifts, hearts, remade hearts, communities,* and *opportunities* all offer vital clues as to how we've been called, each of us, uniquely. For just as God assigns our work, he also equips the workers. Just as he calls us into his work, he also prepares us for it.

So let's learn how to examine these clues.

• • •

OUR GIFTS

God works in the world *through us*—by giving us spiritual gifts. When he calls us to a particular work, he equips us with the proper gifts *for that work*. He's intentional. He doesn't call without equipping, nor does he equip us with gifts he doesn't intend us to use.

The presence (or absence) of a spiritual gift is a strong clue as to our calling. If we possess a particular gift, we can generally assume that we have been or will be called to some sort of work enabled by it. Likewise, if we lack the gifts that enable a particular kind of work, we can generally assume we're not called to that work.*

By examining our spiritual gifts, therefore, we start to get personal; we go a level deeper into *specificity*. We learn about the *how* of our callings, *how* we're meant to love and serve other people.

● ● ●

Consider this question and jot down your response.

B.1   What spiritual gifts did you identify in appendix A? Which ones do you think might be primary gifts? Which ones might be secondary, meant to support your primary ones?

● ● ●

OUR HEARTS

God wires desires, interests, motivations, and ambitions right into our hearts, equipping us to find joy in certain work. From early on certain activities, certain kinds of work, are just more appealing. There are things we look forward to doing. There are others we don't. There are things that interest us, things about which we're naturally curious and about which we love learning. There's work we'd do even if we didn't get paid for it. Work that brings us life.

---

*These are clues not rules. God can be as creative as he wants to be with the timing of things. We might sense our calling before we see or understand our gifts. We might possess a particular gift, for example, but not know it yet and need to develop it over time.

We can even feel a certain compulsion toward it. Sometimes there's work we just cannot *not* do. Narrowing on what he knew, Alexander Graham Bell wrote about this: "Wherever you may find the inventor, you may give him wealth or you may take from him all that he has; and he will go on inventing. He can no more help inventing than he can help thinking or breathing."[1]

The wiring of Bell's heart revealed itself early, before even his teen years. His best friend's family operated a flour mill. He spent time there playing and exploring. But one time, something caught his attention. He somehow noticed the inefficiency of the process by which the mill dehusked wheat. And so, at the age of twelve, he invented something better—a device with spinning paddles and brushes made from nails. The mill used it for many years.

"The place God calls you to is the place where your deep gladness and the world's deep hunger meet," wrote Frederick Buechner (a man with a heart wired for writing, beautifully).[2] We're drawn to certain work because it gives us deep gladness. Bell found it in inventing. It's why he'd work late into the night. He was wired for it.

Notice that the Buechner equation starts with deep gladness, with what makes us come alive, as opposed to starting with the world's deep need. It's because that is what the world needs most. Creation will be rebuilt and restored by God's power but also by men and women who are enthusiastic and interested and joyful and satisfied in their work, not by people slogging through their lives, merely surviving, serving only themselves.

By examining the unique wirings of our unique hearts, we get even more personal. We go deeper yet into *specificity*, deeper into the *how* of our callings.

● ● ●

Consider these questions and jot down your responses.

B.2   What kind of work appeals to you? What kind are you most interested in? What work do you feel compelled to do? What kind brings deep gladness? Make a bulleted list.

B.3   Revisit your list of natural talents from chapter 4. How does it compare to your answers here? Is there overlap?

● ● ●

OUR REMADE HEARTS

God also equips us by *reinventing* our hearts when we begin to trust in Jesus. Just as he did for the people of Israel, he does for us: "I will give you a new heart, and a new spirit I will put within you. And I will remove the heart of stone from your flesh and give you a heart of flesh" (Ezek. 36:26). In this process, we change. Some of our old desires, interests, motivations, and ambitions are wired into our hearts again, but others are not. And some are wired in anew.

You see, these hearts of flesh, our remade hearts, are better at responding to the second half of the Buechner equation. They're better at noticing and addressing the deep needs of the world.

Our remade hearts more closely resemble God's heart. They move more like his moves, and they break more like his breaks. But while they resemble his heart, they're not designed all alike. Nor do they operate all alike. They still reflect our God-created and God-energized individualities.

Notice when you encounter troubling situations, sometimes your heart is moved, deeply. Notice also, sometimes it isn't. Not as deep, at least. Why? Because while we're all created for good works, we aren't created for *every* good work. And while we're all called to help those in need, we aren't called to *every* need.

So the movements of our remade hearts point to what is ours to do. They point us to certain people and places and types of needs. Examining them lets us get even more *personal*, more *specific*. It allows us to get to the *who* of our callings and even the *where*.

● ● ●

Consider this question and jot down your response.

B.4   What needs move your heart? What kinds of people are you drawn to help? What kinds of problems (other people's) are you moved to help solve?

● ● ●

OUR EXPERIENCES

God equips us also by our experiences. The places we've lived; the people who've been significant in our lives, family members, friends; the major and minor events of our lives; the major and minor themes of our stories; our education, our jobs; our failures, our successes; our pain, our joys—God works all these together to prepare us for the work we're meant to do. The apostle Paul wrote this: "For those who love God all things work together for good, for those who are called according to his purpose" (Rom. 8:28).

Often the best place to look is at failures and at our most painful experiences. The lessons learned from them are hard-earned. They can't be learned from books or by hearing other people's stories. That's why *apprentice* is a better analogy than *student*, when exploring identity. Apprentices learn hands-on, by getting their hands dirty, trying things, making mistakes, learning, and then doing better.

And that's often how God teaches us, through our struggles and failures and the hard work of getting through them. We get to see up close how God redeems mistakes, trials, and grief. We get to learn how to respond to Jesus' second commandment—and the second half of the Buechner equation—more appropriately, more powerfully. We gain experience. We gain authority to love and serve others going through their own struggles and failures. We become reliable.

Our experiences, taken by themselves, aren't going to make perfect sense, of course. We cannot see all that God sees. But by examining them, understanding them as best we can, and looking for common themes, we can get even more *personal* and more *specific* about the *how*, *who*, and *where* of our callings.

● ● ●

Consider these questions and jot down your responses.

B.5   Where have you lived; what was your education; what jobs have you held; what people have been most significant in your life; what are the major events of your life, positive and negative; what are the major themes? Spend fifteen to twenty minutes making a bulleted list. Write anything and everything that comes to mind.

B.6   What are the major struggles and failures you've faced? What might give you authority to help others facing similar things? There's nothing too small or insignificant or too deep or traumatic. God can use any part of our story to help others.

● ● ●

OUR COMMUNITIES

Our communities can help us confirm calling, and we need that. Every one of us is prone to mistakes and vulnerable to the influences of culture and the deceits of the Enemy. But God provides for us through wise and Spirit-filled believers who know us. "Speaking the truth in love" (Eph. 4:15) is among the primary tasks of Christian community. When our friends speak to us that way, we're able to "grow up in every way" (v. 15), into true identity and into calling.

Spirit-infused communities are often able to see what we miss or mistake. But we have to be open to hearing them, honestly willing to hear and consider the opinions and wisdom of others.

● ● ●

Consider these questions and jot down your responses.

B.7   What have you heard from other people about your gifts, your talents, or where they've seen you be effective in loving and serving?

B.8   If you haven't, reach out to a trusted friend or mentor, or others in your Christian community. Ask them for their opinion of your calling. What's their response?

B.9   Does the *truth-in-love* from your community support and encourage your conclusions so far? Does it conflict with them in any way? How?

● ● ●

OUR OPPORTUNITIES

We must also pay attention to the opportunities now open to us. The fact that an opportunity is open (or the fact that it has closed) can be an indicator of God's intent.

"God controls seemingly random events," wrote Vern Poythress, the Calvinist thinker and theologian.[3] While it might seem that opportunities open or close according to chance or the whims of others, they actually do so "under God's watchful gaze as part of his eternal plan."[4] When an opportunity opens, God knows about it. He may have opened it himself, but he certainly allowed it to open. Likewise, when an opportunity closes, he knows about that too—and he either closed it himself or allowed it to close.

Job offers, promotions, invitations to volunteer, chunks of time opening up on our calendars—we must pay attention to these things. This is not to say that we should take every opportunity that opens—certainly not. But we must take these things into account, along with everything else, as we move through the calling funnel. Just as we must take it into account when opportunities close or remain closed. For it could be that God's not actually calling us to the work we think he is, or it could be that it's simply not yet time. He could be telling us this: "Not now. Not yet. You need more preparation, more apprenticing."

● ● ●

Consider these questions and jot down your responses.

B.10   What opportunities are open right now that fit with your gifts, your heart, your remade heart, your experiences, and the feedback you've been given by your friends and family?

B.11   What opportunities remain closed?

● ● ●

ONE EXAMPLE

I have a friend, John. He has a mix of three spiritual gifts: teaching, exhortation, and wisdom. When he teaches, encourages, and guides people and organizations, God's work is done. He's also long been drawn to the work of coaching. It's how God, apparently, wired his heart. But then, when he *remade* that heart—at that point when John began following Jesus—God added new wiring that makes John want to come alongside people who don't know God and who lack a strong sense of identity. John now feels compelled to encourage them, teach them about God and themselves, and to help maximize their potential.

As an NFL lineman, John played a key role in the goal line stand that ensured the victory years ago of the San Francisco 49ers over the Cincinnati Bengals in Super Bowl XVI. In the days leading up to that famous game and those just afterward, John got a little glimpse of God's purpose for his life. He knew deep down that the blessing of that win and of being part of that organization—with leaders such as Bill Walsh and Joe Montana—was going to morph into blessings for others through him.

It wasn't just positive experiences that prepared him though. More difficult times did too. His experiences with failure—playing for what was, at the time, one of the worst college football programs in the country, then being taken in the fifth round of the NFL draft, then being cut four times—all worked together to give him humility, sensitivity, and empathy. These experiences gave him authority to coach men and women who are struggling with their own adversity.

Today, John's still learning. He gives his friends permission to speak into his life. We're able to confirm and call out his gifts, talents, and effectiveness. He also seeks feedback from clients of his executive coaching firm.

John's life is an illustration of the calling funnel in action.

Let's take a look:

SCRIPTURE
John's calling is to love and serve other people.

SPIRITUAL GIFTS
The Holy Spirit energizes his spiritual gifts
of teaching, encouraging, and wisdom.

HEART
His heart is wired for coaching; he's drawn to it, and
it brings him deep gladness.

REMADE HEART
His remade heart is wired to help people better
understand God, and better understand themselves
and their potential.

EXPERIENCES
His years in the NFL give him authority to speak
to people about success, failure, teamwork,
leadership, and humility.

COMMUNITY
His community—including the people he
coaches—confirm his gifts, his talents,
and his effectiveness.

OPPORTUNITIES
He's been given the opportunity to run
a firm, coaching business and nonprofit leaders.

CALLING
So this is John's calling (what he knows of it for now, at least): to use the spiritual gifts of
teaching, encouraging, and wisdom to love and serve business leaders by coaching them
into better understandings of God and themselves and their God-given potential.

—— SWITCH ON ——

Narrow the answers you generated above. Pray about them, but again, do it with eyes open and pen in hand. Look at your answers. Listen for God's voice. Let the Holy Spirit guide your thoughts as you consider these questions:

- Does what you wrote feel right, accurate?

- What stands out? What strikes most true?

- Is there anything that, on second look, you might want to reconsider?

- When you look at everything together, can you begin to get a sense of how God's prepared you to love and serve somewhere in this world, uniquely?

- Can you get a sense for what your calling might be?

Pray one more time.

> *God my Father, Jesus my King, Holy Spirit my Counselor, I confess I've sometimes thought very little about others. I confess I've devoted much of my work life on getting what I want, rather than on what other people need. I don't want to be that man anymore. I repent my look-out-for-number-one attitude. I repent my selfishness. I choose to think differently—about myself and about others. I choose a new attitude.*

Thank you for how you've made me—and how you've invited me into your work. Thank you for not forgetting me. Thank you for lifting me up and giving me a place, an important position in your grand work. Thank you for revealing something about that place and that position today. Thank you for my calling. I know I'm not there yet, but I'm ready and willing to be apprenticed into it. Amen.

A WARNING

Alexander Graham Bell's lodging rooms were filled with wires and coils, steel rods and tuning forks, blueprints and batteries. They were messy. Bell and Watson spent countless hours there toiling, trying things, trying to answer questions, failing, and learning. And when they finally succeeded—when Watson finally heard Bell's clear voice—it was amid a bit of chaos. For Bell had bumped a battery and dumped battery acid on himself, and he was calling for assistance. "Mr. Watson. Come here. I want you!"

Workshops are like that. Seeking calling is like that too. It's messy, hard, frustrating, mysterious, wonderful. We'll spend our whole lives seeking it, and there'll always be more to learn. Because we cannot see all God sees. We cannot know all he knows. And we'll never understand ahead of time how things will develop or at what pace.

And that's okay.

This funnel, this process, is not an algorithm. We cannot just plug things in and expect exact answers back. We're not robots. We're made of organic material, and this process is organic too. Some answers may come easily. Others will require faith, patience, and preparation.

So expect give-and-take, trial-and-error. Imagine, if it helps, Bell and Watson. Expect information to be revealed slowly, a bit at a time, and in a sequence—a sequence you won't understand. Expect God to work on a *need-to-know* basis, giving you only the information you need for a given moment. Expect to be frustrated, because your pride is likely to drive you to want to know more sooner; it is likely to drive you to want more clarity than you'll have.

Callings are about specifics—specific work, specific assignments, specific tasks targeted at specific people with specific needs. We don't live in a theoretical world. We live and work in a practical world—a world where we spend every moment doing *something specific*. And as men, we're wired to want to make sure we're spending our moments on the right things.

Jesus, our King, our teacher, our model, nearing the end of his time on earth, prayed this to his Father God:

> I glorified you on earth
> By completing down to the last detail
> What you assigned me to do. (John 17:4 THE MESSAGE)

He didn't say, "I *kinda* did the things you assigned me, more or less" or "I did the *kinds* of things you wanted me to, generally." He said he completed them "down to the last detail." Our frustration—as men who seek to model our lives on the life of Jesus—comes from the fact that we can never know enough about our details. We'll never know all of them, and the ones we do know, we won't know with perfect clarity.

And that's the conundrum of calling.

But here's the really good news. Success in this endeavor, success in seeking calling, is not measured by how much we know. It's measured by *how faithful we are to what we know*.

ILLUSTRATIONS

CHAPTER 002

Edison, Thomas Alva, *Electric-Lamp*, 1880, patent drawing for U.S. Patent 223,989, Google Patents, accessed October 12, 2015, www.google.com/patents/US223898.

United States Department of Energy, *Workers outside of Menlo Park Lab*, 1880, photograph, Wikimedia Foundation, accessed October 12, 2015, https://commons.wikimedia.org/wiki/File:HD.11.031 _(10995366585).jpg.

CHAPTER 003

Kennedy, Rankin, *Marconi Coherer Tube*, 1903, drawing, Wikimedia Foundation, accessed October 12, 2015, https://hu.wikipedia.org /wiki/F%C3%A1jl:Marconi_coherer_tube_(Rankin_Kennedy ,_Electrical_Installations,_Vol_V,_1903).jpg.

Marconi, Guglielmo, *Transmitting Electrical Signals*, 1897, patent drawing for U.S. Patent 586,193, Google Patents, accessed October 12, 2015, www.google.com/patents/US586193.

Marconi Wireless Station, So. Wellfleet, Mass., 1898, digital image, The Miriam and Ira D. Wallach Division of Art, Prints and Photographs: Photography Collection, The New York Public Library: Digital

Collections, accessed October 12, 2015, https://digitalcollections
.nypl.org/items/510d47d9-a3ea-a3d9-e040-e00a18064a99.

CHAPTER 004

Daniels, John T., *Wright Brothers First Successful Flight, Kill Devil
Hills, North Carolina*, 1903, photograph, Wikimedia Foundation,
accessed October 12, 2015, https://en.wikipedia.org/wiki/John_T
._Daniels#/media/File:First_flight2.jpg.

Wright, Orville, and Wilbur Wright, *Flying-machine*, 1911, patent
drawing for U.S. Patent 987,662, Google Patents, accessed October
12, 2015, www.google.com/patents/US987662.

CHAPTER 005

Daguerre, Louis, *Boulevard du Temple, Paris, 3rd Arrondissement*,
1838, photograph, Wikimedia Foundation, accessed October 12,
2015, https://en.wikipedia.org/wiki/File:Boulevard_du_Temple_by
_Daguerre.jpg.

Daguerre, Louis, *Obtaining Daguerreotype Portraits*, 1840, patent
drawing for British Patent 8194.

CHAPTER 006

Bell at the Pemberton Avenue School for the Deaf, 1871, photograph,
Library of Congress Prints and Photographs Division, Wikimedia
Foundation, accessed October 12, 2015, https://commons.wikimedia
.org/wiki/File:Bell_at_the_Pemberton_Avenue_School_for_the
_Deaf,_Boston,_from_the_Library_of_Congress._00837v.jpg.

Bell, Alexander Graham, *Improvement in Telegraphy*, 1876, patent drawing for U.S. Patent 174,465, Google Patents, accessed October 12, 2015, www.google.com/patents/US174465.

CHAPTER 007

Benz & Co. and the Patent-MotorWagen, 1886, photograph, Daimler, accessed October 12, 2015, http://media.daimler.com/marsMedia Site/en/instance/picture.xhtml?oid=7572280.

Benz, Karl, *Vehicle Powered by a Gas Engine*, 1886, patent drawing for German Patent 37435, Wikimedia Foundation, accessed October 12, 2015, https://commons.wikimedia.org/wiki/File:Patentschrift _37435_Benz_Patent-Motorwagen.pdf.

CHAPTER 008

Elisha Otis Demonstration of Free-fall Prevention Mechanism, Crystal Palace, 1854, drawing, Wikimedia Foundation, accessed October 12, 2015, https://commons.wikimedia.org/wiki/File:Elisha_OTIS _1854.jpg.

Otis, Elisha Graves, *Hoisting Apparatus*, 1861, patent drawing for U.S. Patent 31,128, Google Patents, accessed October 12, 2015, www.google.com/patents/US31128.

NOTES

CHAPTER 002

1. John Swansburg, "The Self-Made Man," *Slate*, September 29, 2014, www.slate.com/articles/news_and_politics/history/2014/09/the_self_made_man_history_of_a_myth_from_ben_franklin_to_andrew_carnegie.html.

2. "Electric Lamp," *Thomas A. Edison Papers Project*, Rutgers University, last updated October 28, 2016, http://edison.rutgers.edu/lamp.htm.

3. Dallas Willard, *The Divine Conspiracy: Rediscovering Our Hidden Life in God* (New York: Harper, 1998), 94.

4. Francis Jehl, *Menlo Park Reminiscences* (Dearborn, MI: Edison Institute, 1936), 858.

CHAPTER 003

1. Maria Cristina Marconi, *Marconi My Beloved* (Wellesly, MA: Branden, 2014), 29.

2. Basil Pennington, *Centered Living: The Way of Centering Prayer* (Liguori, MO: Liguori, 2012), Kindle edition.

3. Dallas Willard and Jan Johnson, *Hearing God Through the Year: A 365-Day Devotional* (Westmont, IL: InterVarsity Press, 2004), 275.

4. John Stott, "Evangelism Plus," interview by Tim Stafford, October 13, 2006, www.christianitytoday.com/ct/2006/october/32.94 .html.

5. Dallas Willard, *Hearing God: Developing a Conversational Relationship with God* (Westmont, IL: IVP Books, 2012), 250.

CHAPTER 004

1. Orville Wright, *Papers of Wilbur and Orville Wright, Including the Chanute-Wright Papers*, ed. Marvin McFarland, January 13, 1920 (New York: McGraw-Hill, 1953), papers 1, 3.

2. Fred C. Kelly, *The Wright Brothers: A Biography* (Mineola, NY: Dover, 1989), 101–102.

3. Orville Wright, telegram to his father, December 17, 1903, last updated September 22, 2014, www.wdl.org/en/item/11372/.

4. A. W. Tozer, "Gifts of the Spirit 2" (sermon, Chicago, IL, 1956).

5. Timothy Keller, "Participating in God's Work," *Daily Keller: Wisdom from Tim Keller 365 Days a Year* (blog), January 31, 2015, http://dailykeller.com/participating-in-gods-work/.

6. A. W. Tozer, *Keys to the Deeper Life* (Grand Rapids, MI: Zondervan, 1964), 57.

CHAPTER 005

1. Samuel F. B. Morse, letter, *New York Observer*, April 20, 1839.

2. Amanda Uren, "1838: The First Photograph of a Human Being," *Mashable*, accessed June 27, 2019, http://mashable.com/2014/11/05/first-photograph-of-a-human/.

3. George MacDonald, "The New Name: Unspoken Sermons Series One," *Christian Classics Ethereal Library*, accessed June 27, 2019, www.ccel.org/ccel/macdonald/unspoken1.vi.html.

4. Eric S. Raymond, *The New Hacker's Dictionary* (Cambridge, MA: The MIT Press, 1996), 208.

5. Matthew Henry, *Matthew Henry's Concise Commentary on the Whole Bible* (Nashville: Thomas Nelson, 2003), 53.

6. John Ortberg, "You Have a Calling" (sermon, Menlo Park, CA, 2006).

7. John Eldredge, *The New Name*, 2011, John Eldredge and Ransomed Heart Ministries, MP3 recording.

CHAPTER 006

1. Charlotte Gray, *Reluctant Genius: Alexander Graham Bell and the Passion for Invention* (New York: Arcade, 2006), 267.

2. Gray, *Reluctant Genius*, 84.

3. Gray, *Reluctant Genius*, 92.

4. Gray, *Reluctant Genius*, 122.

5. Naomi Pasachoff, *Alexander Graham Bell* (Oxford, UK: Oxford University Press, 1996), 131.

6. N. T. Wright, *Surprised by Hope: Rethinking Heaven, the Resurrection, and the Mission of the Church* (San Francisco: HarperOne, 2008), 200.

7. C. S. Lewis, *The Problem of Pain* (London: The Macmillan Company, 1944), 47.

8. A. Roy Petrie, *Alexander Graham Bell* (Ontario, Canada: Fitzhenry & Whiteside, 1975), 17.

9. Mack Douglas, *How to Make a Habit of Succeeding* (Gretna, LA: Pelican, 1994), 26.

10. Robert Bruce, *Bell: Alexander Graham Bell and the Conquest of Solitude* (Ithaca, NY: Cornell University Press, 1990), 209.

11. A. W. Tozer, *The Pursuit of God* (Abbotsford, WI: Aneko, 2015), 110.

CHAPTER 007

1. "August 1888: Bertha Benz Takes World's First Long-Distance Trip in an Automobile," 2016, Daimler, http://media.daimler.com/marsMediaSite/en/instance/ko/August-1888-Bertha-Benz-takes-worldsfirst-long-distance-tri.xhtml?oid=9361401.

2. Timothy Keller, *Every Good Endeavor: Connecting Your Work to God's Work* (New York: Penguin, 2012), 39.

3. C. S. Lewis, *Mere Christianity* (San Francisco: HarperOne, 2015), 51.

4. C. S. Lewis, *The Screwtape Letters* (San Francisco: HarperOne, 2015), 63.

5. Charles Spurgeon, *Lectures to my Students* (New York: Sheldon & Company, 1875), 260.

6. David Edman Gray, *Practicing Balance: How Congregations Can Support Harmony in Work and Life* (Lanham, MD: Rowman & Littlefield, 2012), 77.

CHAPTER 008

1. Frederick Buechner, *Beyond Words: Daily Readings in the ABCs of Faith* (San Francisco: HarperOne, 2004), 139.

2. Charles Spurgeon, "Our Gifts and How to Use Them" (sermon, London, 1872).

3. Thomas Merton, *New Seeds of Contemplation* (New York: New Directions, 1961), 31.

APPENDIX A

1. Oswald Chambers, *Christian Disciplines: Building Strong Character through Divine Guidance, Suffering, Peril, Prayer, Loneliness, and Patience* (Grand Rapids, MI: Discovery House, 2013), Kindle edition.

2. A. W. Tozer, "Gifts of the Spirit 1" (sermon, Chicago, IL, 1956).

3. Philip Yancey, *Prayer: Does It Make Any Difference?* (Grand Rapids, MI: Zondervan, 2006), 257.

4. Dallas Willard, *Hearing God: Developing a Conversational Relationship with God* (Westmont, IL: IVP Books, 2012), 65.

5. Dallas Willard and John Ortberg, "A Conversation on Pain and Suffering," November 2011, Menlo Park, CA.

APPENDIX B

1. Judith Tulloch, *The Bell Family in Baddeck: Alexander Graham Bell and Mabel Bell in Cape Breton* (Halifax, Canada: Formac, 2006), 75.

2. Frederick Buechner, *Wishful Thinking: A Seeker's ABC* (San Francisco: HarperOne, 1993), 95.

3. Vern S. Poythress, *Chance and the Sovereignty of God: A God-Centered Approach to Probability and Random Events* (Wheaton, IL: Crossway, 2014), 34.

4. Poythress, Chance *and the Sovereignty of God*, back cover.

ACKNOWLEDGMENTS

Thank you to Jennifer, my wife and dearest friend. How could I doubt God's love when I get to share my life with a person like you?

Thank you to Heather and C. J. Fitzgerald, our great friends and biggest champions. Without your financial support, nothing we do at Gather Ministries would be possible.

Thank you to the men of the Table. My friends. My brothers. The men who know me and love me still. I'm so grateful for how you fight for me, and I'm honored to fight for each one of you. Thank you also to the men of the Cave, who first taught me how to seek identity.

Thank you to everyone who took time to read early versions, including C. J. Fitzgerald, Kevin Hartley, Jim Candy, Mike Benkert, Gilbert Ahrens, Robert Pietsch, Terel Beppu, Patrick Wilkinson, and John Ortberg. I will never forget your generosity.

Thank you to Paul Pastor, a fearless editor, a super-smart wordsmith, and a good friend. Your patience, encouragement, and wisdom were blessings to this project.

Thank you to Mark Russell and Wendi Lord, who each believed in the vision and fought for this book.

Thank you to my parents, Nannette and Jerome Camp, who taught me about love and who had my back—no matter what.

Thank you to our amazing mentors, John and Stasi Eldredge. Thank you for your love and guidance and wisdom.

And to my King, my Best Friend, my Savior, thank you. Thank you for choosing me. Thank you for giving me a place and a position. Thank you for loving me. Thank you for helping me love you, right back.

ABOUT THE AUTHOR

Justin is a co-founder of Gather Ministries, a nonprofit he runs with his wife, Jennifer. He wrote *WiRE: A One-Year, Twice-a-Week Devotional for Busy Men.*

Justin also co-founded a seed-stage venture capital firm, through which he had the opportunity to invest in some amazing Silicon Valley entrepreneurs. Prior to that, he was a lawyer in New York City.

Justin, Jennifer, and their three children live on the San Francisco Peninsula.

Made in the USA
Monee, IL
11 April 2021